TROILUS AND CRESSIDA

TROILUS
AND CRESSIDA

William Shakespeare

WORDSWORTH CLASSICS

The paper in this book is produced from pure wood
pulp, without the use of chlorine or any other substance
harmful to the environment. The energy used in its
production consists almost entirely of hydroelectricity
and heat generated from waste materials, thereby
conserving fossil fuels and contributing little to the
greenhouse effect.

This edition published 1993 by
Wordsworth Editions Limited
Cumberland House, Crib Street, Ware,
Hertfordshire SG12 9ET

ISBN 1 85326 083 5

Printed and bound by Clays Ltd, St Ives PLC
Typeset in the UK by The R & B Partnership

Introduction

THE THEME OF THE TROJAN WAR has exercised a perennial fascination for writers from earliest times. The inevitable tragedy of the Fall of Troy is made more poignant by the events and personalities which precede it; the abduction of Helen by Paris, the pride and the gallantry of the military heroes, the cunning of Ulysses and the doomed prophesies of the hapless Cassandra.

The scene is set by an armed Prologue who explains the convocation of the proud princes on the Trojan plain. The play opens in Troy outside King Priam's palace where his son Troilus is in conversation with the artful Pandarus, the uncle to Cressida with whom Troilus is in love. Pandarus agrees to contrive a meeting between the young prince and Cressida, and this is eventually effected. At first, Cressida resists Troilus' advances, but in time she admits her love for him, and this love is duly consummated. Meanwhile, the war continues with discord and plotting among the Greeks, but they manage to recruit to their side Calchas, a Trojan priest who is Cressida's father. As reward for his betrayal of Troy, Calchas demands that during a routine exchange of prisoners his daughter should be brought to him so that he can bestow her on Diomedes, a Greek commander. Protestations of undying love accompany the exchange of lovegifts as the two lovers are parted. Cressida's initiation into the delights of love has so delighted her that she falls easy prey to the Greek charm of Diomedes, and when Troilus sees her give his love-token to her new lover he knows that he is betrayed. 'Let all pitiful goers-between be called to the world's end after my name – call them Pandars: let all constant men be Troiluses, all false women Cressids'.

Troilus and Cressida is generally considered one of Shakespeare's 'problem plays'. No high moral value is preached by the play, nor is it light enough to be regarded as a straight comedy. The twin themes of sexual and political betrayal co-exist, but Troilus and the Trojans are seen as highminded dupes, while the more pragmatic Greeks make their mistakes too. (One is tempted to view them as Sellars and Yeatman regarded the combatants in the English Civil War: 'The Cavaliers were Wrong but Wromantic, the Roundheads Right but Repulsive'). The play contains some of Shakespeare's more explicit eroticism in the exchanges between the two protagonists, and in the bawdy exchanges of Pandarus and the scurrilous Thyrsites. The play is based on Chaucer's *Troilus and Criseyde*, itself an adaptation of Boccaccio's *Il Filostrato*. But Shakespeare seems to have been familiar with Lygate's *Siege of Troy* (c1420) and Caxton's *Recuyell of the Histories of Troy* (1474). The story of Troilus and Cressida first emerged in medieval times, and has no basis in classical antiquity. The play was probably written in 1602 for performance in one of the Inns of Court.

Details of Shakespeare's early life are scanty. He was the son of a prosperous merchant of Stratford-upon-Avon, and tradition has it that he was born on 23rd April 1564; records show that he was baptised three days later. It is likely that he attended the local grammar school, but he had no university education. Of his early career there is no record, though John Aubrey states that he was, for a time, a country schoolmaster. How he became involved with the stage is equally uncertain, but he was sufficiently established as a playwright by 1592 to be criticised in print. He was a leading member of the Lord Chamberlain's Company, which became the King's Men on the accession of James I in 1603. Shakespeare married Anne Hathaway in 1582, by whom he had two daughters and a son, Hamnet, who died in childhood. Towards the end of his life he loosened his ties with London, and retired to New Place, his substantial property in Stratford that he had bought in 1597. He died on 23rd April 1616 aged 52, and is buried in Holy Trinity Church, Stratford.

Further reading:

R Kimborough: Shakespeare's 'Troilus and Cressida' and its Setting 1964
W W Lawrence: Shakespeare's Problem Comedies 1931, 1969
E Partridge: Shakespeare's Bawdy 1947, rev 1955
E M W Tillyard: Shakespeare's Problem Plays 1950

Troilus and Cressida

The scene: Troy, and the Greek camp

CHARACTERS IN THE PLAY

PRIAM, *king of Troy*
HECTOR
TROILUS
PARIS } *his sons*
DEIPHOBUS
HELENUS
MARGARELON, *a bastard son of Priam*
ÆNEAS
ANTENOR } *Trojan commanders*
CALCHAS, *a Trojan priest, taking part with the Greeks*
PANDARUS, *uncle to Cressida*
AGAMEMNON, *the Greek general*
MENELAUS, *his brother*
ACHILLES
AJAX
ULYSSES
NESTOR } *Greek commanders*
DIOMEDES
PATROCLUS
THERSITES, *a deformed and scurrilous Greek*
ALEXANDER, *servant to Cressida*
Servant to Troilus
Servant to Paris
Servant to Diomedes
The Prologue

HELEN, *wife to Menelaus*
ANDROMACHE, *wife to Hector*
CASSANDRA, *daughter to Priam; a prophetess*
CRESSIDA, *daughter to Calchas*

Trojan and Greek Soldiers, and Attendants

TROILUS AND CRESSIDA

Enter the Prologue in armour

Prologue. In Troy there lies the scene. From isles
    of Greece
The princes orgulous, their high blood chafed,
Have to the port of Athens sent their ships,
Fraught with the ministers and instruments
Of cruel war; sixty and nine, that wore
Their crownets regal, from th'Athenian bay
Put forth toward Phrygia, and their vow is made
To ransack Troy, within whose strong immures
The ravished Helen, Menelaus' queen,
With wanton Paris sleeps—and that's the quarrel.   10
To Tenedos they come,
And the deep-drawing barks do there disgorge
Their warlike fraughtage; now on Dardan plains
The fresh and yet unbruised Greeks do pitch
Their brave pavilions: Priam's six-gated city,
Dardan, and Timbria, Helias, Chetas, Troien,
And Antenorides, with massy staples
And corresponsive and fulfilling bolts,
Sperr up the sons of Troy.
Now expectation, tickling skittish spirits   20
On one and other side, Trojan and Greek,
Sets all on hazard—and hither am I come
A Prologue armed, but not in confidence
Of author's pen or actor's voice, but suited
In like condition as our argument,
To tell you, fair beholders, that our play
Leaps o'er the vaunt and firstlings of those broils,

Beginning in the middle; starting thence away
To what may be digested in a play.
30 Like or find fault; do as your pleasures are:
Now good or bad, 'tis but the chance of war.   [*goes*

[1. 1.]   *Troy. Before Priam's palace*

Enter PANDARUS *and* TROILUS *in armour*

Troilus. Call here my varlet; I'll unarm again:
Why should I war without the walls of Troy
That find such cruel battle here within?
Each Trojan that is master of his heart,
Let him to field; Troilus, alas, hath none!
Pandarus. Will this gear ne'er be mended?
Troilus. The Greeks are strong, and skilful to
    their strength,
Fierce to their skill, and to their fierceness valiant,
But I am weaker than a woman's tear,
10 Tamer than sleep, fonder than ignorance,
Less valiant than the virgin in the night,
And skilless as unpractised infancy.
Pandarus. Well, I have told you enough of this; for
my part, I'll not meddle nor make no farther. He that
will have a cake out of the wheat must tarry the
grinding.
Troilus. Have I not tarried?
Pandarus. Ay, the grinding; but you must tarry the
bolting.
20 *Troilus.* Have I not tarried?
Pandarus. Ay, the bolting; but you must tarry the
leavening.
Troilus. Still have I tarried.

Pandarus. Ay, to the leavening; but there's yet in the
word hereafter, the kneading, the making of the cake,
the heating of the oven, and the baking; nay, you must
stay the cooling too, or you may chance to burn your
lips.

Troilus. Patience herself, what goddess e'er she be,
Doth lesser blench at sufferance than I do;   30
At Priam's royal table do I sit,
And when fair Cressid comes into my thoughts—
So, traitor! 'When she comes!'—When is she thence?

Pandarus. Well, she looked yesternight fairer than
ever I saw her look, or any woman else.

Troilus. I was about to tell thee—when my heart,
As wedgéd with a sigh, would rive in twain,
Lest Hector or my father should perceive me,
I have, as when the sun doth light a storm,
Buried this sigh in wrinkle of a smile: 40
But sorrow that is couched in seeming gladness
Is like that mirth fate turns to sudden sadness.

Pandarus. An her hair were not somewhat darker
than Helen's—well, go to—there were no more comparison between the women. But, for my part, she is
my kinswoman; I would not, as they term it, praise her,
but I would somebody had heard her talk yesterday,
as I did. I will not dispraise your sister Cassandra's
wit, but—

Troilus. O Pandarus! I tell thee, Pandarus—   50
When I do tell thee there my hopes lie drowned,
Reply not in how many fathoms deep
They lie indrenched. I tell thee I am mad
In Cressid's love. Thou answer'st she is fair;
Pour'st in the open ulcer of my heart
Her eyes, her hair, her cheek, her gait, her voice;
Handlest in thy discourse—O, that her hand,

In whose comparison all whites are ink
Writing their own reproach, to whose soft seizure
60 The cygnet's down is harsh, and spirit of sense
Hard as the palm of ploughman! this thou tell'st me,
As true thou tell'st me, when I say I love her;
But saying thus, instead of oil and balm,
Thou lay'st in every gash that love hath given me
The knife that made it.

Pandarus. I speak no more than truth.

Troilus. Thou dost not speak so much.

Pandarus. Faith, I'll not meddle in 't. Let her be as
she is. If she be fair, 'tis the better for her; an she be
70 not, she has the mends in her own hands.

Troilus. Good Pandarus, how now, Pandarus!

Pandarus. I have had my labour for my travail:
ill thought on of her, and ill thought on of you; gone
between and between, but small thanks for my labour.

Troilus. What, art thou angry, Pandarus? what,
with me?

Pandarus. Because she's kin to me, therefore she's not
so fair as Helen; an she were not kin to me, she would
be as fair o' Friday as Helen is o' Sunday. But what
care I? I care not an she were a blackamoor; 'tis all
80 one to me.

Troilus. Say I she is not fair?

Pandarus. I do not care whether you do or no.
She's a fool to stay behind her father. Let her to the
Greeks, and so I'll tell her the next time I see her. For
my part, I'll meddle nor make no more i'th' matter.

Troilus. Pandarus—

Pandarus. Not I.

Troilus. Sweet Pandarus—

Pandarus. Pray you, speak no more to me: I will
90 leave all as I found it, and there an end. [*goes; alarum*

Troilus. Peace, you ungracious clamours! peace,
  rude sounds!
Fools on both sides! Helen must needs be fair,
When with your blood you daily paint her thus.
I cannot fight upon this argument;
It is too starved a subject for my sword.
But Pandarus—O gods, how do you plague me!
I cannot come to Cressid but by Pandar,
And he's as tetchy to be wooed to woo
As she is stubborn-chaste against all suit.
Tell me, Apollo, for thy Daphne's love,   100
What Cressid is, what Pandar, and what we?
Her bed is India; there she lies, a pearl;
Between our Ilium and where she resides
Let it be called the wild and wandering flood;
Ourself the merchant, and this sailing Pandar,
Our doubtful hope, our convoy and our bark.

Alarum. Enter ÆNEAS

Æneas. How now, Prince Troilus! Wherefore
  not afield?
Troilus. Because not there; this woman's answer sorts,
For womanish it is to be from thence.
What news, Æneas, from the field today?   110
Æneas. That Paris is returnéd home, and hurt.
Troilus. By whom, Æneas?
Æneas.   Troilus, by Menelaus.
Troilus. Let Paris bleed: 'tis but a scar to scorn;
Paris is gored with Menelaus' horn.   [*alarum*
Æneas. Hark what good sport is out of town today!
Troilus. Better at home, if 'would I might' were 'may'.
But to the sport abroad: are you bound thither?
Æneas. In all swift haste.
Troilus.   Come, go we then together. [*they go*

[1. 2.]   *The same. A street*

Enter CRESSIDA *and* ALEXANDER, *her man*

Cressida. Who were those went by?
Alexander.   .   Queen Hecuba and Helen.
Cressida. And whither go they?
Alexander.   Up to the eastern tower,
Whose height commands as subject all the vale,
To see the battle. Hector, whose patience
Is as a virtue fixed, today was moved:
He chid Andromache and struck his armourer;
And, like as there were husbandry in war,
Before the sun rose he was harnessed light,
And to the field goes he; where every flower
10 Did, as a prophet, weep what it foresaw
In Hector's wrath.
Cressida.   What was his cause of anger?
Alexander. The noise goes this: there is among
        the Greeks
A lord of Trojan blood, nephew to Hector;
They call him Ajax.
Cressida.   Good; and what of him?
Alexander. They say he is a very man per se,
And stands alone.
Cressida. So do all men, unless they are drunk, sick,
or have no legs.
Alexander.. This man, lady, hath robbed many beasts
20 of their particular additions: he is as valiant as the lion,
churlish as the bear, slow as the elephant—a man into
whom nature hath so crowded humours that his valour
is crushed into folly, his folly forced with discretion.
There is no man hath a virtue that he hath not a glimpse
of, nor any man an attaint but he carries some stain of

it; he is melancholy without cause and merry against
the hair; he hath the joints of everything, but everything so out of joint that he is a gouty Briareus, many
hands and no use, or a purblind Argus, all eyes and
no sight.   30

Cressida. But how should this man, that makes me
smile, make Hector angry?

Alexander. They say he yesterday coped Hector in
the battle and struck him down, the disdain and shame
whereof hath ever since kept Hector fasting and waking.

Cressida. Who comes here?

Alexander. Madam, your uncle Pandarus.

Enter PANDARUS

Cressida. Hector's a gallant man.

Alexander. As may be in the world, lady.

Pandarus. What's that? what's that?   40

Cressida. Good morrow, uncle Pandarus.

Pandarus. Good morrow, cousin Cressid. What do
you talk of? Good morrow, Alexander. How do you,
cousin? When were you at Ilium?

Cressida. This morning, uncle.

Pandarus. What were you talking of when I came?
Was Hector armed and gone ere you came to Ilium?
Helen was not up, was she?

Cressida. Hector was gone; but Helen was not up.

Pandarus. E'en so: Hector was stirring early.   50

Cressida. That were we talking of, and of his anger.

Pandarus. Was he angry?

Cressida. So he says here.

Pandarus. True, he was so; I know the cause too;
he'll lay about him today, I can tell them that. And
there's Troilus will not come far behind him; let them
take heed of Troilus, I can tell them that too.

Cressida. What, is he angry too?

Pandarus. Who, Troilus? Troilus is the better man
60 of the two.

Cressida. O Jupiter! there's no comparison.

Pandarus. What, not between Troilus and Hector?
Do you know a man if you see him?

Cressida. Ay, if I ever saw him before and knew him.

Pandarus. Well, I say Troilus is Troilus.

Cressida. Then you say as I say; for I am sure he is
not Hector.

Pandarus. No, nor Hector is not Troilus in some
degrees.

70 *Cressida.* 'Tis just to each of them; he is himself.

Pandarus. Himself! Alas, poor Troilus! I would he
were—

Cressida. So he is.

Pandarus. Condition I had gone barefoot to India.

Cressida. He is not Hector.

Pandarus. Himself! no, he's not himself. Would
'a were himself! Well, the gods are above; time must
friend or end. Well, Troilus, well, I would my heart
were in her body! No, Hector is not a better man than
80 Troilus.

Cressida. Excuse me.

Pandarus. He is elder.

Cressida. Pardon me, pardon me.

Pandarus. Th'other's not come to't. You shall tell me
another tale when th'other's come to't. Hector shall
not have his wit this year.

Cressida. He shall not need it, if he have his own.

Pandarus. Nor his qualities.

Cressida. No matter.

90 *Pandarus.* Nor his beauty.

Cressida. 'Twould not become him; his own's better.

Pandarus. You have no judgement, niece. Helen herself swore th'other day that Troilus for a brown favour, for so 'tis, I must confess—not brown neither—

Cressida. No, but brown.

Pandarus. Faith, to say the truth, brown and not brown.

Cressida. To say the truth, true and not true.

Pandarus. She praised his complexion above Paris.

Cressida. Why, Paris hath colour enough.   100

Pandarus. So he has.

Cressida. Then Troilus should have too much: if she praised him above, his complexion is higher than his; he having colour enough, and the other higher, is too flaming a praise for a good complexion. I had as lief Helen's golden tongue had commended Troilus for a copper nose.

Pandarus. I swear to you, I think Helen loves him better than Paris.

Cressida. Then she's a merry Greek indeed.   110

Pandarus. Nay, I am sure she does. She came to him th'other day into the compassed window—and, you know, he has not past three or four hairs on his chin—

Cressida. Indeed, a tapster's arithmetic may soon bring his particulars therein to a total.

Pandarus. Why, he is very young; and yet will he within three pound lift as much as his brother Hector.

Cressida. Is he so young a man and so old a lifter?

Pandarus. But to prove to you that Helen loves him: she came and puts me her white hand to his cloven 120 chin—

Cressida. Juno have mercy! how came it cloven?

Pandarus. Why, you know, 'tis dimpled. I think his smiling becomes him better than any man in all Phrygia.

Cressida. O, he smiles valiantly.

Pandarus. Does he not?

Cressida. O yes, an 'twere a cloud in autumn.

Pandarus. Why, go to, then! But to prove to you that Helen loves Troilus—

130 *Cressida.* Troilus will stand to the proof, if you'll prove it so.

Pandarus. Troilus! Why, he esteems her no more than I esteem an addle egg.

Cressida. If you love an addle egg as well as you love an idle head, you would eat chickens i'th'shell.

Pandarus. I cannot choose but laugh to think how she tickled his chin; indeed, she has a marvellous white hand, I must needs confess—

Cressida. Without the rack.

140 *Pandarus.* And she takes upon her to spy a white hair on his chin.

Cressida. Alas, poor chin! many a wart is richer.

Pandarus. But there was such laughing! Queen Hecuba laughed, that her eyes ran o'er.

Cressida. With millstones.

Pandarus. And Cassandra laughed.

Cressida. But there was a more temperate fire under the pot of her eyes. Did her eyes run o'er too?

Pandarus. And Hector laughed.

150 *Cressida.* At what was all this laughing?

Pandarus. Marry, at the white hair that Helen spied on Troilus' chin.

Cressida. An't had been a green hair, I should have laughed too.

Pandarus. They laughed not so much at the hair as at his pretty answer.

Cressida. What was his answer?

Pandarus. Quoth she, 'Here's but two and fifty hairs on your chin, and one of them is white'.

Cressida. This is her question.   160

Pandarus. That's true; make no question of that.
'Two and fifty hairs', quoth he, 'and one white; that
white hair is my father, and all the rest are his sons.'
'Jupiter!' quoth she, 'which of these hairs is Paris my
husband?' 'The forked one,' quoth he; 'pluck't out,
and give it him.' But there was such laughing, and
Helen so blushed, and Paris so chafed, and all the rest
so laughed, that it passed!

Cressida. So let it now; for it has been a great while
going by.   170

Pandarus. Well, cousin, I told you a thing yesterday;
think on't.

Cressida. So I do.

Pandarus. I'll be sworn 'tis true; he will weep you an
'twere a man born in April.

Cressida. And I'll spring up in his tears an 'twere a
nettle against May.   [*retreat sounded*

Pandarus. Hark! they are coming from the field.
Shall we stand up here and see them as they pass toward
Ilion? Good niece, do, sweet niece Cressida.   180

Cressida. At your pleasure.

Pandarus. Here, here, here's an excellent place; here
we may see most bravely. I'll tell you them all by their
names as they pass by. But mark Troilus above the rest.

Cressida. Speak not so loud.

ÆNEAS passes

Pandarus. That's Æneas. Is not that a brave man?
He's one of the flowers of Troy, I can tell you. But
mark Troilus; you shall see Troilus anon.

ANTENOR passes

Cressida. Who's that?

Pandarus. That's Antenor. He has a shrewd wit, 190

I can tell you, and he's a man good enough: he's one
o'th' soundest judgements in Troy whosoever, and a
proper man of person. When comes Troilus? I'll show
you Troilus anon. If he see me, you shall see him nod
at me.

 Cressida. Will he give you the nod?

 Pandarus. You shall see.

 Cressida. If he do, the rich shall have more.

HECTOR passes

 Pandarus. That's Hector, that, that, look you, that;
200 there's a fellow! Go thy way, Hector! There's a brave
man, niece. O brave Hector! Look how he looks!
There's a countenance! Is't not a brave man?

 Cressida. O, a brave man!

 Pandarus. Is 'a not? It does a man's heart good. Look
you what hacks are on his helmet! Look you yonder,
do you see? look you there: there's no jesting; there's
laying on, take't off who will, as they say; there be
hacks!

 Cressida. Be those with swords?

210 *Pandarus.* Swords! anything, he cares not; an the
devil come to him, it's all one. By God's lid, it does
one's heart good. Yonder comes Paris, yonder comes
Paris.

PARIS passes

Look ye yonder, niece; is't not a gallant man too, is't not?
Why, this is brave now. Who said he came home hurt
today? He's not hurt. Why, this will do Helen's heart
good now, ha! Would I could see Troilus now! You
shall see Troilus anon.

HELENUS passes

 Cressida. Who's that?

Pandarus. That's Helenus. I marvel where Troilus 220
is. That's Helenus. I think he went not forth today.
That's Helenus.

Cressida. Can Helenus fight, uncle?

Pandarus. Helenus! no—yes, he'll fight indifferent
well. I marvel where Troilus is. Hark! do you not
hear the people cry 'Troilus'? Helenus is a priest.

Cressida. What sneaking fellow comes yonder?

TROILUS passes

Pandarus. Where? yonder? that's Deiphobus. 'Tis
Troilus! there's a man, niece! Hem! Brave Troilus! the
prince of chivalry! 230

Cressida. Peace, for shame, peace!

Pandarus. Mark him; note him. O brave Troilus!
Look well upon him, niece; look you how his sword is
bloodied, and his helm more hacked than Hector's, and
how he looks, and how he goes! O admirable youth!
he ne'er saw three and twenty. Go thy way, Troilus,
go thy way! Had I a sister were a grace, or a daughter
a goddess, he should take his choice. O admirable man!
Paris? Paris is dirt to him; and, I warrant, Helen, to
change, would give an eye to boot. 240

Common Soldiers pass

Cressida. Here come more.

Pandarus. Asses, fools, dolts! chaff and bran, chaff and
bran! porridge after meat! I could live and die i' th'
eyes of Troilus. Ne'er look, ne'er look; the eagles are
gone: crows and daws, crows and daws! I had rather
be such a man as Troilus than Agamemnon and all
Greece.

Cressida. There is among the Greeks Achilles, a
better man than Troilus.

2-2

250 *Pandarus.* Achilles! a drayman, a porter, a very camel.
Cressida. Well, well.
Pandarus. Well, well! Why, have you any discretion?
have you any eyes? do you know what a man is? Is not
birth, beauty, good shape, discourse, manhood, learning,
gentleness, virtue, youth, liberality, and such like, the
spice and salt that season a man?
Cressida. Ay, a minced man; and then to be baked
with no date in the pie, for then the man's date is out.
Pandarus. You are such another woman, a man
260 knows not at what ward you lie.
Cressida. Upon my back, to defend my belly; upon
my wit, to defend my wiles; upon my secrecy, to defend
mine honesty; my mask, to defend my beauty; and you,
to defend all these: and at all these wards I lie, at a
thousand watches.
Pandarus. Say one of your watches.
Cressida. Nay, I'll watch you for that; and that's one
of the chiefest of them too: if I cannot ward what I
would not have hit, I can watch you for telling how
270 I took the blow; unless it swell past hiding, and then
it's past watching.
Pandarus. You are such another!

Enter Troilus' Boy

Boy. Sir, my lord would instantly speak with you.
Pandarus. Where?
Boy. At your own house; there he unarms him.
Pandarus. Good boy, tell him I come. [*Boy goes*]
I doubt he be hurt. Fare ye well, good niece.
Cressida. Adieu, uncle.
Pandarus. I'll be with you, niece, by and by.
280 *Cressida.* To bring, uncle?
Pandarus. Ay, a token from Troilus.

Cressida. By the same token, you are a bawd.

[*Pandarus goes*

Words, vows, gifts, tears, and love's full sacrifice,
He offers in another's enterprise;
But more in Troilus thousandfold I see
Than in the glass of Pandar's praise may be.
Yet hold I off: women are angels, wooing;
Things won are done—joy's soul lies in the doing.
That she beloved knows nought that knows not this:
Men prize the thing ungained more than it is.   290
That she was never yet that ever knew
Love got so sweet as when desire did sue.
Therefore this maxim out of love I teach:
'Achievement is command; ungained, beseech.'
Then though my heart's content firm love doth bear,
Nothing of that shall from mine eyes appear. [*they go*

[1. 3.]   *The Greek camp. Before Agamemnon's tent*

Sennet. Enter AGAMEMNON, NESTOR, ULYSSES,
MENELAUS, with others

Agamemnon. Princes,
What grief hath set this jaundice on your cheeks?
The ample proposition that hope makes   ·
In all designs begun on earth below
Fails in the promised largeness: checks
        and disasters
Grow in the veins of actions highest reared,
As knots, by the conflux of meeting sap,
Infect the sound pine and divert his grain
Tortive and errant from his course of growth.
Nor, princes, is it matter new to us   10

That we come short of our suppose so far
That after seven years' siege yet Troy walls stand;
Sith every action that hath gone before
Whereof we have record, trial did draw
Bias and thwart, not answering the aim
And that unbodied figure of the thought
That gave't surmiséd shape. Why then, you princes,
Do you with cheeks abashed behold our works,
And call them shames, which are indeed nought else
20 But the protractive trials of great Jove
To find persistive constancy in men?
The fineness of which metal is not found
In fortune's love: for then the bold and coward,
The wise and fool, the artist and unread,
The hard and soft, seem all affined and kin;
But, in the wind and tempest of her frown,
Distinction with a broad and powerful fan,
Puffing at all, winnows the light away,
And what hath mass or matter, by itself
30 Lies rich in virtue and unmingléd.
    Nestor. With due observance of thy godlike seat,
Great Agamemnon, Nestor shall apply
Thy latest words. In the reproof of chance
Lies the true proof of men: the sea being smooth,
How many shallow bauble boats dare sail
Upon her patient breast, making their way
With those of nobler bulk!
But let the ruffian Boreas once enrage
The gentle Thetis, and anon behold
40 The strong-ribbed bark through liquid mountains cut,
Bounding between the two moist elements
Like Perseus' horse; where's then the saucy boat
Whose weak untimbered sides but even now
Co-rivalled greatness?—either to harbour fled,

Or made a toast for Neptune. Even so
Doth valour's show and valour's worth divide
In storms of fortune: for in her ray and brightness
The herd hath more annoyance by the breese
Than by the tiger; but when the splitting wind
Makes flexible the knees of knotted oaks   50
And flies flee under shade, why then the thing of courage,
As roused with rage, with rage doth sympathize,
And with an accent tuned in selfsame key
Retorts to chiding fortune.
    Ulysses.   Agamemnon,
Thou great commander, nerve and bone of Greece,
Heart of our numbers, soul and only spirit,
In whom the tempers and the minds of all
Should be shut up, hear what Ulysses speaks.
Besides th'applause and approbation
The which, [*to Agamemnon*] most mighty for thy place
    and sway,   60
[*to Nestor*] And thou most reverend for thy stretched-
    out life,
I give to both your speeches, which were such
As, Agamemnon, all the hands of Greece
Should hold up high in brass, and such again
As, venerable Nestor, hatched in silver,
Should with a bond of air, strong as the axletree
On which heaven rides, knit all the Greekish ears
To his experienced tongue—yet let it please both,
Thou great, and wise, to hear Ulysses speak.
    Agamemnon. Speak, Prince of Ithaca; and be't of
        less expect   70
That matter needless, of importless burden,
Divide thy lips than we are confident,
When rank Thersites opes his mastic jaws,
We shall hear music, wit and oracle.

Ulysses. Troy, yet upon his basis, had been down,
And the great Hector's sword had lacked a master,
But for these instances:
The specialty of rule hath been neglected;
And look how many Grecian tents do stand
80 Hollow upon this plain, so many hollow factions.
When that the general is not like the hive
To whom the foragers shall all repair,
What honey is expected? Degree being vizarded,
Th'unworthiest shows as fairly in the mask.
The heavens themselves, the planets, and this centre,
Observe degree, priority, and place,
Insisture, course, proportion, season, form,
Office, and custom, in all line of order;
And therefore is the glorious planet Sol
90 In noble eminence enthroned and sphered
Amidst the other; whose medicinable eye
Corrects the influence of evil planets,
And posts, like the commandment of a king,
Sans check to good and bad. But when the planets
In evil mixture to disorder wander,
What plagues and what portents, what mutiny,
What raging of the sea, shaking of earth,
Commotion in the winds, frights, changes, horrors,
Divert and crack, rend and deracinate
100 The unity and married calm of states
Quite from their fixure! O, when degree is shaked,
Which is the ladder of all high designs,
The enterprise is sick! How could communities,
Degrees in schools, and brotherhoods in cities,
Peaceful commerce from dividable shores,
The primogenitive and due of birth,
Prerogative of age, crowns, sceptres, laurels,
But by degree, stand in authentic place?

Take but degree away, untune that string,
And hark what discord follows! each thing meets   110
In mere oppugnancy: the bounded waters
Should lift their bosoms higher than the shores,
And make a sop of all this solid globe;
Strength should be lord of imbecility,
And the rude son should strike his father dead;
Force should be right; or rather, right and wrong,
Between whose endless jar justice resides,
Should lose their names, and so should justice too.
Then everything includes itself in power,
Power into will, will into appetite;   120
And appetite, an universal wolf,
So doubly seconded with will and power,
Must make perforce an universal prey,
And last eat up himself. Great Agamemnon,
This chaos, when degree is suffocate,
Follows the choking.
And this neglection of degree it is
That by a pace goes backward, with a purpose
It hath to climb. The general's disdained
By him one step below, he by the next,   130
That next by him beneath; so every step,
Exampled by the first pace that is sick
Of his superior, grows to an envious fever
Of pale and bloodless emulation—
And 'tis this fever that keeps Troy on foot,
Not her own sinews: to end a tale of length,
Troy in our weakness stands, not in her strength.
 Nestor. Most wisely hath Ulysses here discovered
The fever whereof all our power is sick.
 Agamemnon. The nature of the sickness found, Ulysses,   140
What is the remedy?
 Ulysses. The great Achilles, whom opinion crowns

The sinew and the forehand of our host,
Having his ear full of his airy fame,
Grows dainty of his worth, and in his tent
Lies mocking our designs. With him, Patroclus,
Upon a lazy bed, the livelong day
Breaks scurril jests,
And with ridiculous and awkward action,
150 Which, slanderer, he imitation calls,
' He pageants us. Sometime, great Agamemnon,
Thy topless deputation he puts on,
And, like a strutting player whose conceit
Lies in his hamstring, and doth think it rich
To hear the wooden dialogue and sound
'Twixt his stretched footing and the scaffoldage,
Such to-be-pitied and o'er-wrested seeming
He acts thy greatness in; and, when he speaks,
'Tis like a chime a-mending; with terms unsquared,
160 Which, from the tongue of roaring Typhon dropped,
Would seem hyperboles. At this fusty stuff,
The large Achilles, on his pressed bed lolling,
From his deep chest laughs out a loud applause,
Cries 'Excellent! 'tis Agamemnon right!
Now play me Nestor: hem, and stroke thy beard,
As he being dressed to some oration.'
That's done—as near as the extremest ends
Of parallels, as like as Vulcan and his wife.
Yet god Achilles still cries 'Excellent!
170 'Tis Nestor right! Now play him me, Patroclus,
Arming to answer in a night alarm.'
And then, forsooth, the faint defects of age
Must be the scene of mirth: to cough and spit,
And, with a palsy fumbling on his gorget,
Shake in and out the rivet. And at this sport
Sir Valour dies; cries 'O, enough, Patroclus,

Or give me ribs of steel! I shall split all
In pleasure of my spleen!' And in this fashion,
All our abilities, gifts, natures, shapes,
Severals and generals of grace exact,   180
Achievements, plots, orders, preventions,
Excitements to the field or speech for truce,
Success or loss, what is or is not, serves .
As stuff for these two to make paradoxes.
    Nestor. And in the imitation of these twain,
Who, as Ulysses says, opinion crowns
-With an imperial voice, many are infect.
Ajax is grown self-willed and bears his head
In such a rein, in full as proud a place
As broad Achilles; keeps his tent like him;   190
Makes factious feasts; rails on our state of war
Bold as an oracle; and sets Thersites,
A slave whose gall coins slanders like a mint,
To match us in comparisons with dirt,
To weaken and discredit our exposure,
How rank soever rounded in with danger.
    Ulysses. They tax our policy and call it cowardice,
Count wisdom as no member of the war, ‹
Forestall prescience, and esteem no act
But that of hand; the still and mental parts   200
That do contrive how many hands shall strike
When fitness calls them on, and know by measure
Of their observant toil the enemy's weight—
Why, this hath not a finger's dignity:
They call this bed-work, mappery, closet-war;
So that the ram that batters down the wall,
For the great swing and rudeness of his poise,
They place before his hand that made the engine
Or those that with the fineness of their souls
By reason guide his execution.   210

Nestor. Let this be granted, and Achilles' horse
Makes many Thetis' sons.   [*tucket*
  Agamemnon. What trumpet? look, Menelaus.
  Menelaus. From Troy.

Enter ÆNEAS

  Agamemnon. What would you 'fore our tent?
  Æneas. Is this great Agamemnon's tent, I pray you?
  Agamemnon. Even this.
  Æneas. May one that is a herald and a prince
Do a fair message to his kingly eyes?
220 *Agamemnon.* With surety stronger than Achilles' arms
'Fore all the Greekish heads, which with one voice
Call Agamemnon head and general.
  Æneas. Fair leave and large security. How may
A stranger to those most imperial looks
Know them from eyes of other mortals?
  Agamemnon.   How?
  Æneas. Ay:
I ask, that I might waken reverence,
And bid the cheek be ready with a blush
Modest as morning when she coldly eyes
230 The youthful Phoebus.
Which is that god in office, guiding men?
Which is the high and mighty Agamemnon?
  Agamemnon. This Trojan scorns us, or the men
        of Troy
Are ceremonious courtiers.
  Æneas. Courtiers as free, as debonair, unarmed,
As bending angels: that's their fame in peace.
But when they would seem soldiers, they have galls,
Good arms, strong joints, true swords, and—
     Jove's accord—
Nothing so full of heart. But peace, Æneas,

Peace, Trojan; lay thy finger on thy lips!   240
The worthiness of praise distains his worth,
If that the praised himself bring the praise forth:
But what the repining enemy commends,
That breath fame blows; that praise, sole
  pure, transcends.
 Agamemnon. Sir you of Troy, call you
  yourself Æneas?
 Æneas. Ay, Greek, that is my name.
 Agamemnon. What's your affair, I pray you?
 Æneas. Sir, pardon: 'tis for Agamemnon's ears.
 Agamemnon. He hears nought privately that comes
  from Troy.
 Æneas. Nor I from Troy come not to whisper him; 250
I bring a trumpet to awake his ear,
To set his sense on the attentive bent,
And then to speak.
 Agamemnon.   Speak frankly as the wind;
It is not Agamemnon's sleeping hour.
That thou shalt know, Trojan, he is awake,
He tells thee so himself.
 Æneas.   Trumpet, blow loud,
Send thy brass voice through all these lazy tents;
And every Greek of mettle, let him know,
What Troy means fairly shall be spoke aloud.
       [trumpet sounds
We have, great Agamemnon, here in Troy 260
A prince called Hector—Priam is his father—
Who in this dull and long-continued truce
Is resty grown. He bade me take a trumpet,
And to this purpose speak: kings, princes, lords!
If there be one among the fair'st of Greece,
That holds his honour higher than his ease,
That seeks his praise more than he fears his peril,

That knows his valour and knows not his fear,
That loves his mistress more than in confession
270 With truant vows to her own lips he loves,
And dare avow her beauty and her worth
In other arms than hers—to him this challenge!
Hector, in view of Trojans and of Greeks,
Shall make it good, or do his best to do it,
He hath a lady, wiser, fairer, truer,
Than ever Greek did couple in his arms;
And will tomorrow with his trumpet call
Midway between your tents and walls of Troy,
To rouse a Grecian that is true in love.
280 If any come, Hector shall honour him;
If none, he'll say in Troy when he retires,
The Grecian dames are sunburnt and not worth
The splinter of a lance. Even so much.
    Agamemnon. This shall be told our lovers, Lord Æneas.
If none of them have soul in such a kind,
We left them all at home. But we are soldiers;
And may that soldier a mere recreant prove,
That means not, hath not, or is not in love!
If then one is, or hath, or means to be,
290 That one meets Hector; if none else, I am he.
    Nestor. Tell him of Nestor, one that was a man
When Hector's grandsire sucked. He is old now;
But if there be not in our Grecian host
One noble man that hath one spark of fire,
To answer for his love, tell him from me
I'll hide my silver beard in a gold beaver
And in my vantbrace put this withered brawn,
And, meeting him, will tell him that my lady
Was fairer than his grandam and as chaste
300 As may be in the world: his youth in flood,
    I'll prove this truth with my three drops of blood.

Æneas. Now heavens forfend such scarcity of youth!
Ulysses. Amen.
Agamemnon. Fair Lord Æneas, let me touch
    your hand;
To our pavilion shall I lead you first.
Achilles shall have word of this intent;
So shall each lord of Greece, from tent to tent.
Yourself shall feast with us before you go,
And find the welcome of a noble foe.
                 [they go; Ulysses detains Nestor
  Ulysses. Nestor!   310
  Nestor. What says Ulysses?
  Ulysses. I have a young conception in my brain;
Be you my time to bring it to some shape.
  Nestor. What is't?
  Ulysses. This 'tis:
Blunt wedges rive hard knots; the seeded pride
That hath to this maturity blown up
In rank Achilles must or now be cropped,
Or, shedding, breed a nursery of like evil
To overbulk us all.
  Nestor.   Well, and how?   320
  Ulysses. This challenge that the gallant Hector sends,
However it is spread in general name,
Relates in purpose only to Achilles.
  Nestor. True: the purpose is perspicuous
    as substance,
Whose grossness little characters sum up;
And, in the publication, make no strain
But that Achilles, were his brain as barren
As banks of Libya—though, Apollo knows,
'Tis dry enough—will, with great speed of judgement,
Ay, with celerity, find Hector's purpose   330
Pointing on him.

Ulysses. And wake him to the answer, think you?
Nestor. Why, 'tis most meet. Who may you
    else oppose
That can from Hector bring his honour off,
If not Achilles? Though't be a sportful combat,
Yet in this trial much opinion dwells:
For here the Trojans taste our dear'st repute
With their fin'st palate—and trust to me, Ulysses,
Our imputation shall be oddly poised
340 In this wild action; for the success,
Although particular, shall give a scantling
Of good or bad unto the general;
And in such indexes, although small pricks
To their subsequent volumes, there is seen
The baby figure of the giant mass
Of things to come at large. It is supposed
He that meets Hector issues from our choice;
And choice, being mutual act of all our souls,
Makes merit her election, and doth boil,
350 As 'twere from forth us all, a man distilled
Out of our virtues; who miscarrying,
What heart receives from hence a conquering part,
To steel a strong opinion to themselves?
Which entertained, limbs are his instruments,
E'en no less working than are swords and bows
Directive by the limbs.
    Ulysses. Give pardon to my speech: therefore 'tis meet
Achilles meet not Hector. Let us, like merchants,
First show foul wares, and think perchance they'll sell.
360 If not, the lustre of the better shall exceed
By showing the worse first. Do not consent
That ever Hector and Achilles meet;
For both our honour and our shame in this
Are dogged with two strange followers.

Nestor. I see them not with my old eyes: what
     are they?
Ulysses. What glory our Achilles shares
     from Hector,
Were he not proud, we all should share with him.
But he already is too insolent;
And we were better parch in Afric sun
Than in the pride and salt scorn of his eyes,   370
Should he scape Hector fair: if he were foiled,
Why, then we did our main opinion crush
In taint of our best man. No, make a lottery,
And by device let blockish Ajax draw
The sort to fight with Hector; 'mong ourselves
Give him allowance as the better man;
For that will physic the great Myrmidon,
Who broils in loud applause, and make him fall
His crest that prouder than blue Iris bends.
If the dull brainless Ajax come safe off,   380
We'll dress him up in voices; if he fail,
Yet go we under our opinion still
That we have better men. But, hit or miss,
Our project's life this shape of sense assumes—
Ajax employed plucks down Achilles' plumes.
     Nestor. Ulysses,
Now I begin to relish thy advice,
And I will give a taste thereof forthwith
To Agamemnon. Go we to him straight.
Two curs shall tame each other: pride alone   390
Must tarre the mastiffs on, as 'twere their bone.
                                        [*they go*

[2. 1.]   *The Greek camp*

Enter AJAX *and* THERSITES

Ajax. Thersites!

Thersites. Agamemnon—how if he had boils, full, all over, generally?

Ajax. Thersites!

Thersites. And those boils did run? Say so: did not the general run then? were not that a botchy core?

Ajax. Dog!

Thersites. Then would come some matter from him; I see none now.

10 *Ajax.* Thou bitch-wolf's son, canst thou not hear? Feel, then.   [*strikes him*

Thersites. The plague of Greece upon thee, thou mongrel beef-witted lord!

Ajax. Speak then, thou vinewed'st leaven, speak! I will beat thee into handsomeness!

Thersites. I shall sooner rail thee into wit and holiness; but I think thy horse will sooner con an oration than thou learn a prayer without book. Thou canst strike, canst thou? A red murrain o' thy jade's tricks!

20 *Ajax.* Toadstool, learn me the proclamation.

Thersites. Dost thou think I have no sense, thou strikest me thus?

Ajax. The proclamation!

Thersites. Thou art proclaimed a fool, I think.

Ajax. Do not, porpentine, do not; my fingers itch.

Thersites. I would thou didst itch from head to foot and I had the scratching of thee; I would make thee the loathsomest scab in Greece. When thou art forth in the incursions, thou strikest as slow as another.

30 *Ajax.* I say, the proclamation!

Thersites. Thou grumblest and railest every hour on Achilles, and thou art as full of envy at his greatness as Cerberus is at Proserpina's beauty, ay, that thou barkest at him.

Ajax. Mistress Thersites!

Thersites. Thou shouldst strike him.

Ajax. Cobloaf!

Thersites. He would pun thee into shivers with his fist, as a sailor breaks a biscuit.

Ajax. You whoreson cur!   [*strikes him* 40

Thersites. Do, do, thou stool for a witch! ay, do, do, thou sodden-witted lord! Thou hast no more brain in thy head than I have in mine elbows; an assinego may tutor thee. Thou scurvy-valiant ass! thou art here but to thrash Trojans; and thou art bought and sold among those of any wit, like a barbarian slave. If thou use to beat me, I will begin at thy heel and tell what thou art by inches, thou thing of no bowels, thou!

Ajax. You dog!

Thersites. You scurvy lord!   50

Ajax. You cur!   [*strikes him*

Thersites. Mars his idiot! do, rudeness; do, camel, do, do.

Enter ACHILLES and PATROCLUS

Achilles. Why, how now, Ajax! Wherefore do you thus? How now, Thersites! What's the matter, man?

Thersites. You see him there, do you?

Achilles. Ay; what's the matter?

Thersites. Nay, look upon him.

Achilles. So I do; what's the matter?

Thersites. Nay, but regard him well.   60

Achilles. 'Well!'—why, so I do.

Thersites. But yet you look not well upon him: for whosoever you take him to be, he is Ajax.

Achilles. I know that, fool.

Thersites. Ay, but that fool knows not himself.

Ajax. Therefore I beat thee.

Thersites. Lo, lo, lo, lo, what modicums of wit he utters! His evasions have ears thus long. I have bobbed his brain more than he has beat my bones. I will buy
70 nine sparrows for a penny, and his pia mater is not worth the ninth part of a sparrow. This lord, Achilles— Ajax, who wears his wit in his belly and his guts in his head—I'll tell you what I say of him.

Achilles. What?

Thersites. I say this Ajax— [*Ajax offers to strike him*

Achilles. Nay, good Ajax.

Thersites. Has not so much wit—

Achilles. Nay, I must hold you.

Thersites. As will stop the eye of Helen's needle, for
80 whom he comes to fight.

Achilles. Peace, fool!

Thersites. I would have peace and quietness, but the fool will not—he there; that he; look you there!

Ajax. O thou damned cur! I shall—

Achilles. Will you set your wit to a fool's?

Thersites. No, I warrant you; for the fool's will shame it.

Patroclus. Good words, Thersites.

Achilles. What's the quarrel?
90 *Ajax.* I bade the vile owl go learn me the tenour of the proclamation, and he rails upon me.

Thersites. I serve thee not.

Ajax. Well, go to, go to.

Thersites. I serve here voluntary.

Achilles. Your last service was sufferance, 'twas not voluntary. No man is beaten voluntary. Ajax was here the voluntary, and you as under an impress.

Thersites. E'en so; a great deal of your wit too lies in your sinews, or else there be liars. Hector shall have a great catch an 'a knock out either of your brains: 'a were 100 as good crack a fusty nut with no kernel.

Achilles. What, with me too, Thersites?

Thersites. There's Ulysses and old Nestor, whose wit was mouldy ere your grandsires had nails on their toes, yoke you like draught-oxen, and make you plough up the wars.

Achilles. What? what?

Thersites. Yes, good sooth: to, Achilles! to, Ajax, to!

Ajax. I shall cut out your tongue.

Thersites. 'Tis no matter; I shall speak as much wit 110 as thou afterwards.

Patroclus. No more words, Thersites; peace!

Thersites. I will hold my peace when Achilles' brach bids me, shall I?

Achilles. There's for you, Patroclus.

Thersites. I will see you hanged, like clotpolls, ere I come any more to your tents. I will keep where there is wit stirring, and leave the faction of fools.   [*goes*

Patroclus. A good riddance.

Achilles. Marry, this, sir, is proclaimed through all
          our host: 120
That Hector, by the fifth hour of the sun,
Will with a trumpet 'twixt our tents and Troy
Tomorrow morning call some knight to arms
That hath a stomach, and such a one that dare
Maintain—I know not what; 'tis trash. Farewell.

Ajax. Farewell. Who shall answer him?

Achilles. I know not. 'Tis put to lottery; otherwise
He knew his man.

Ajax. O, meaning you. I'll go learn more of it.
                                                              [*they go*

[2. 2.]   *Troy. Priam's palace*

Enter PRIAM, HECTOR, TROILUS, PARIS,
and HELENUS

Priam. After so many hours, lives, speeches spent,
Thus once again says Nestor from the Greeks:
'Deliver Helen, and all damage else—
As honour, loss of time, travail, expense,
Wounds, friends, and what else dear that
      is consumed
In hot digestion of this cormorant war—
Shall be struck off.' Hector, what say you to't?
  Hector. Though no man lesser fears the Greeks
      than I
As far as toucheth my particular,
10 Yet, dread Priam,
There is no lady of more softer bowels,
More spongy to suck in the sense of fear,
More ready to cry out 'Who knows what follows?'
Than Hector is. The wound of peace is surety,
Surety secure; but modest doubt is called
The beacon of the wise, the tent that searches
To th'bottom of the worst. Let Helen go.
Since the first sword was drawn about this question,
Every tithe-soul 'mongst many thousand dismes
20 Hath been as dear as Helen—I mean, of ours.
If we have lost so many tenths of ours
To guard a thing not ours, nor worth to us—
Had it our name—the value of one ten,
What merit's in that reason which denies
The yielding of her up?
  Troilus.   Fie, fie, my brother!
Weigh you the worth and honour of a king
So great as our dread father in a scale

Of common ounces? Will you with counters sum
The past-proportion of his infinite,
And buckle in a waist most fathomless 30
With spans and inches so diminutive
As fears and reasons? Fie, for godly shame!
 Helenus. No marvel though you bite so sharp
  at reasons,
You are so empty of them. Should not our father
Bear the great sway of his affairs with reasons,
Because your speech hath none that tells him so?
 Troilus. You are for dreams and slumbers,
  brother priest.
You fur your gloves with reasons. Here are
  your reasons:
You know an enemy intends you harm;
You know a sword employed is perilous, 40
And reason flies the object of all harm;
Who marvels then, when Helenus beholds
A Grecian and his sword, if he do set
The very wings of reason to his heels
And fly, like chidden Mercury from Jove
Or like a star disorbed? Nay, if we talk of reason,
Let's shut our gates and sleep. Manhood
  and honour
Should have hare hearts, would they but fat
  their thoughts
With this crammed reason; reason and respect
Make livers pale and lustihood deject. 50
 Hector. Brother, she is not worth what she doth cost
The keeping.
 Troilus. What's aught, but as 'tis valued?
 Hector. But value dwells not in particular will:
It holds his estimate and dignity
As well wherein 'tis precious of itself

As in the prizer. 'Tis mad idolatry
To make the service greater than the god;
And the will dotes that is attributive
To what infectiously itself affects,
60 Without some image of th'affected merit.
   Troilus. I take today a wife, and my election
Is led on in the conduct of my will;
My will enkindled by mine eyes and ears—
Two traded pilots 'twixt the dangerous shores
Of will and judgement—how may I avoid,
Although my will distaste what it elected,
The wife I chose? There can be no evasion
To blench from this and to stand firm by honour.
We turn not back the silks upon the merchant
70 When we have soiled them; nor the remainder viands
We do not throw in unrespective sieve
Because we now are full. It was thought meet
Paris should do some vengeance on the Greeks;
Your breath of full consent bellied his sails;
The seas and winds, old wranglers, took a truce,
And did him service; he touched the ports desired;
And for an old aunt whom the Greeks held captive
He brought a Grecian queen, whose youth
    and freshness
Wrinkles Apollo's and makes pale the morning.
80 Why keep we her?—the Grecians keep our aunt;
Is she worth keeping?—why, she is a pearl
Whose price hath launched above a thousand ships
And turned crowned kings to merchants.
If you'll avouch 'twas wisdom Paris went—
As you must needs, for you all cried 'Go, go';
If you'll confess he brought home worthy prize—
As you must needs, for you all clapped your hands
And cried 'Inestimable!'; why do you now

The issue of your proper wisdoms rate,
And do a deed that Fortune never did, 90
Beggar the estimation which you prized
Richer than sea and land? O, theft most base,
That we have stolen what we do fear to keep!
But thieves unworthy of a thing so stolen,
That in their country did them that disgrace
We fear to warrant in our native place!
 Cassandra [*within*]. Cry, Trojans, cry!
 Priam.   What noise, what shriek is this?
 Troilus. 'Tis our mad sister, I do know her voice.
 Cassandra [*within*]. Cry, Trojans!
 Hector. It is Cassandra. 100

Enter CASSANDRA, *raving, with her hair
about her ears*

 Cassandra. Cry, Trojans, cry! lend me ten
  thousand eyes,
And I will fill them with prophetic tears.
 Hector. Peace, sister, peace!
 Cassandra. Virgins and boys, mid-age and
  wrinkled eld,
Soft infancy, that nothing canst but cry,
Add to my clamours! Let us pay betimes
A moiety of that mass of moan to come.
Cry, Trojans, cry! Practise your eyes with tears!
Troy must not be, nor goodly Ilion stand;
Our firebrand brother, Paris, burns us all. 110
Cry, Trojans, cry! a Helen and a woe:
Cry, cry! Troy burns, or else let Helen go. [*goes*
 Hector. Now youthful Troilus, do not these
  high strains
Of divination in our sister work
Some touches of remorse, or is your blood

So madly hot that no discourse of reason,
Nor fear of bad success in a bad cause,
Can qualify the same?
 Troilus.   Why, brother Hector,
We may not think the justness of each act
120 Such and no other than event doth form it,
Nor once deject the courage of our minds
Because Cassandra's mad. Her brainsick raptures
Cannot distaste the goodness of a quarrel
Which hath our several honours all engaged
To make it gracious. For my private part,
I am no more touched than all Priam's sons;
And Jove forbid there should be done amongst us
Such things as might offend the weakest spleen
To fight for and maintain!
130 *Paris*. Else might the world convince of levity
As well my undertakings as your counsels;
But I attest the gods, your full consent
Gave wings to my propension and cut off
All fears attending on so dire a project.
For what, alas, can these my single arms?
What propugnation is in one man's valour
To stand the push and enmity of those
This quarrel would excite? Yet, I protest,
Were I alone to pass the difficulties
140 And had as ample power as I have will,
Paris should ne'er retract what he hath done,
Nor faint in the pursuit.
 Priam.   Paris, you speak
Like one besotted on your sweet delights;
You have the honey still, but these the gall:
So to be valiant is no praise at all.
 Paris. Sir, I propose not merely to myself
The pleasures such a beauty brings with it,

But I would have the soil of her fair rape
Wiped off in honourable keeping her.
What treason were it to the ransacked queen,   150
Disgrace to your great worths, and shame to me,
Now to deliver her possession up
On terms of base compulsion! Can it be
That so degenerate a strain as this
Should once set footing in your generous bosoms?
There's not the meanest spirit on our party
Without a heart to dare or sword to draw
When Helen is defended; nor none so noble
Whose life were ill bestowed or death unfamed
Where Helen is the subject. Then, I say,   160
Well may we fight for her whom we know well
The world's large spaces cannot parallel.
  Hector. Paris and Troilus, you have both said well,
And on the cause and question now in hand
Have glozed—but superficially; not much
Unlike young men, whom Aristotle thought
Unfit to hear moral philosophy.
The reasons you allege do more conduce
To the hot passion of distempered blood
Than to make up a free determination   170
'Twixt right and wrong: for pleasure and revenge
Have ears more deaf than adders to the voice
Of any true decision. Nature craves
All dues be rendered to their owners: now,
What nearer debt in all humanity
Than wife is to the husband? If this law
Of nature be corrupted through affection,
And that great minds, of partial indulgence
To their benuméd wills, resist the same,
There is a law in each well-ordered nation   180
To curb those raging appetites that are

Most disobedient and refractory.
If Helen then be wife to Sparta's king,
As it is known she is, these moral laws
Of nature and of nations speak aloud
To have her back returned. Thus to persist
In doing wrong extenuates not wrong,
But makes it much more heavy. Hector's opinion
Is this in way of truth. Yet, ne'ertheless,
190 My sprightly brethren, I propend to you
In resolution to keep Helen still;
For 'tis a cause that hath no mean dependence
Upon our joint and several dignities.
    Troilus. Why, there you touched the life of
      our design:
Were it not glory that we more affected
Than the performance of our heaving spleens,
I would not wish a drop of Trojan blood
Spent more in her defence. But, worthy Hector,
She is a theme of honour and renown,
200 A spur to valiant and magnanimous deeds,
Whose present courage may beat down our foes,
And fame in time to come canonize us;
For I presume brave Hector would not lose
So rich advantage of a promised glory
As smiles upon the forehead of this action
For the wide world's revenue.
    Hector.   I am yours,
You valiant offspring of great Priamus.
I have a roisting challenge sent amongst
The dull and factious nobles of the Greeks
210 Will strike amazement to their drowsy spirits.
I was advertised their great general slept,
Whilst emulation in the army crept:
This, I presume, will wake him.   *[they go*

[2. 3.]   *The Greek camp.   Before the tent*
of Achilles

Enter THERSITES, *solus*

Thersites. How now, Thersites! What, lost in the
labyrinth of thy fury! Shall the elephant Ajax carry it
thus? He beats me, and I rail at him. O worthy
satisfaction! Would it were otherwise: that I could
beat him, whilst he railed at me. 'Sfoot, I'll learn to
conjure and raise devils but I'll see some issue of my
spiteful execrations. Then there's Achilles—a rare
enginer. If Troy be not taken till these two undermine
it, the walls will stand till they fall of themselves.
O thou great thunder-darter of Olympus, forget that   10
thou art Jove, the king of gods, and, Mercury, lose all
the serpentine craft of thy caduceus, if ye take not that
little little less than little wit from them that they have!
which short-armed ignorance itself knows is so abun-
dant scarce, it will not in circumvention deliver a fly
from a spider without drawing their massy irons and
cutting the web. After this, the vengeance on the whole
camp! or, rather, the Neapolitan bone-ache! for that,
methinks, is the curse dependent on those that war for
a placket. I have said my prayers; and devil Envy say   20
'Amen'. What ho! my Lord Achilles!

Patroclus [*within*]. Who's there? Thersites? Good
Thersites, come in and rail.

Thersites. If I could a' remembered a gilt counterfeit,
thou wouldst not have slipped out of my contempla-
tion; but it is no matter—thyself upon thyself! The
common curse of mankind, folly and ignorance, be
thine in great revenue! Heaven bless thee from a tutor,
and discipline come not near thee! Let thy blood be

30 thy direction till thy death! Then if she that lays thee
out says thou art a fair corpse, I'll be sworn and sworn
upon't she never shrouded any but lazars. Amen.

Enter PATROCLUS

Where's Achilles?

Patroclus. What, art thou devout? Wast thou in
prayer?

Thersites. Ay; the heavens hear me!

Patroclus. Amen.

Achilles [*within*]. Who's there?

Patroclus. Thersites, my lord.

Enter ACHILLES

40 *Achilles.* Where, where? O where? Art thou come?
Why, my cheese, my digestion, why hast thou not
served thyself in to my table so many meals? Come,
what's Agamemnon?

Thersites. Thy commander, Achilles; then tell me,
Patroclus, what's Achilles?

Patroclus. Thy lord, Thersites; then tell me, I pray
thee, what's thyself?

Thersites. Thy knower, Patroclus; then tell me,
Patroclus, what art thou?

50 *Patroclus.* Thou mayst tell that knowest.

Achilles. O tell, tell.

Thersites. I'll decline the whole question. Agamemnon commands Achilles; Achilles is my lord; I am
Patroclus' knower, and Patroclus is a fool.

Patroclus. You rascal!

Thersites. Peace, fool! I have not done.

Achilles. He is a privileged man. Proceed, Thersites.

Thersites. Agamemnon is a fool; Achilles is a fool;
Thersites is a fool, and, as aforesaid, Patroclus is a fool.

Achilles. Derive this; come. · 60

Thersites. Agamemnon is a fool to offer to command Achilles; Achilles is a fool to be commanded of Agamemnon; Thersites is a fool to serve such a fool; and Patroclus is a fool positive.

Patroclus. Why am I a fool?

Thersites. Make that demand of the Creator. It suffices me thou art. Look you, who comes here?

Achilles. Patroclus, I'll speak with nobody. Come in with me, Thersites.   [*enters his tent*

Thersites. Here is such patchery, such juggling and 70 such knavery! All the argument is a whore and a cuckold—a good quarrel to draw emulous factions and bleed to death upon. Now, the dry serpigo on the subject, and war and lechery confound all!

[*enters the tent*

Enter AGAMEMNON, ULYSSES, NÉSTOR,
  DIOMEDES, and AJAX

Agamemnon. Where is Achilles?

Patroclus. Within his tent; but ill-disposed, my lord.

Agamemnon. Let it be known to him that we are here.
We sent our messengers, and we lay by
Our appertainments, visiting of him.
Let him be told so, lest perchance he think   80
We dare not move the question of our place,
Or know not what we are.

Patroclus.   I shall say so to him.   [*goes in*

Ulysses. We saw him at the opening of his tent:
He is not sick.

Ajax. Yes, lion-sick, sick of proud heart. You may call it melancholy, if you will favour the man; but, by my head, 'tis pride. But why, why? Let him show us the cause. A word, my lord.   [*takes Agamemnon aside*

Nestor. What moves Ajax thus to bay at him?

90   *Ulysses.* Achilles hath inveigled his fool from him.

Nestor. Who, Thersites?

Ulysses. He.

Nestor. Then will Ajax lack matter, if he have lost his argument.

Ulysses. No, you see, he is his argument that has his argument—Achilles.

Nestor. All the better: their fraction is more our wish than their faction. But it was a strong composure a fool could disunite!

100 *Ulysses.* The amity that wisdom knits not, folly may easily untie.

Re-enter PATROCLUS

Here comes Patroclus.

Nestor. No Achilles with him.

Ulysses. The elephant hath joints, but none for courtesy: his legs are legs for necessity, not for flexure.

Patroclus. Achilles bids me say he is much sorry
If anything more than your sport and pleasure
Did move your greatness and this noble state
To call upon him; he hopes it is no other
110 But for your health and your digestion's sake,
An after-dinner's breath.

Agamemnon.   Hear you, Patroclus:
We are too well acquainted with these answers;
But his evasion, winged thus swift with scorn,
Cannot outfly our apprehensions.
Much attribute he hath, and much the reason
Why we ascribe it to him; yet all his virtues,
Not virtuously on his own part beheld,
Do in our eyes begin to lose their gloss,
Yea, like fair fruit in an unwholesome dish,
120 Are like to rot untasted. Go and tell him

We come to speak with him; and you shall not sin
If you do say we think him over-proud
And under-honest, in self-assumption greater
Than in the note of judgement; and worthier
    than himself
Here tend the savage strangeness he puts on,
Disguise the holy strength of their command,
And underwrite in an observing kind
His humorous predominance; yea, watch
His pettish lunes, his ebbs and flows, as if
The passage and whole carriage of this action   130
Rode on his tide. Go tell him this, and add
That if he overhold his price so much
We'll none of him but let him, like an engine
Not portable, lie under this report:
'Bring action hither; this cannot go to war:
A stirring dwarf we do allowance give
Before a sleeping giant.' Tell him so.

    Patroclus. I shall; and bring his answer presently.
                             [enters the tent
    Agamemnon. In second voice we'll not be satisfied;
We come to speak with him. Ulysses, enter you.   140
                           [Ulysses follows

    Ajax. What is he more than another?
    Agamemnon. No more than what he thinks he is.
    Ajax. Is he so much? Do you not think he thinks
himself a better man than I am?
    Agamemnon. No question.
    Ajax. Will you subscribe his thought and say he is?
    Agamemnon. No, noble Ajax; you are as strong, as
valiant, as wise, no less noble, much more gentle, and
altogether more tractable.
    Ajax. Why should a man be proud? How doth pride 150
grow? I know not what pride is.

   4

Agamemnon. Your mind is the clearer, Ajax, and your virtues the fairer. He that is proud eats up himself: pride is his own glass, his own trumpet, his own chronicle; and whatever praises itself but in the deed, devours the deed in the praise.

Ajax. I do hate a proud man as I do hate the engendering of toads.

(*Nestor.* And yet he loves himself: is it not strange?

Re-enter ULYSSES

160   *Ulysses.* Achilles will not to the field tomorrow.

Agamemnon. What's his excuse?

Ulysses.   He doth rely on none,
But carries on the stream of his dispose
Without observance or respect of any,
In will peculiar and in self-admission.

Agamemnon. Why will he not, upon our fair request,
Untent his person and share th'air with us?

Ulysses. Things small as nothing, for request's
          sake only,
He makes important; possessed he is with greatness,
And speaks not to himself but with a pride
170   That quarrels at self-breath: imagined worth
Holds in his blood such swollen and hot discourse
That 'twixt his mental and his active parts
Kingdomed Achilles in commotion rages
And batters down himself. What should I say?
He is so plaguey proud that the death-tokens of it
Cry 'No recovery'.

Agamemnon.   Let Ajax go to him.
Dear lord, go you and greet him in his tent.
'Tis said he holds you well, and will be led,
At your request, a little from himself.

180   *Ulysses.* O Agamemnon, let it not be so!

We'll consecrate the steps that Ajax makes
When they go from Achilles. Shall the proud lord
That bastes his arrogance with his own seam
And never suffers matter of the world
Enter his thoughts, save such as doth revolve
And ruminate himself, shall he be worshipped
Of that we hold an idol more than he?
No, this thrice-worthy and right valiant lord
Must not so stale his palm, nobly acquired,
Nor, by my will, assubjugate his merit—   190
As amply titled as Achilles is—
By going to Achilles:
That were to enlard his fat-already pride,
And add more coals to Cancer when he burns
With entertaining great Hyperion.
This lord go to him! Jupiter forbid,
And say in thunder 'Achilles go to him'.
  (Nestor. O, this is well; he rubs the vein of him.
  (Diomedes. And how his silence drinks up
      this applause!
  Ajax. If I go to him, with my arméd fist   200
I'll pash him o'er the face.
  Agamemnon. O, no, you shall not go.
  Ajax. An 'a be proud with me, I'll feeze his pride:
Let me go to him.
  Ulysses. Not for the worth that hangs upon
      our quarrel.
  Ajax. A paltry, insolent fellow!
  (Nestor. How he describes himself!
  Ajax. Can he not be sociable?
  (Ulysses. The raven chides blackness.
  Ajax. I'll let his humour's blood.   210
  (Agamemnon. He will be the physician that should be
the patient.

4-2

Ajax. An all men were o' my mind—

(*Ulysses.* Wit would be out of fashion.

Ajax. 'A should not bear it so; 'a should eat swords first. Shall pride carry it?

(*Nestor.* An 'twould, you'ld carry half.

(*Ulysses.* 'A would have ten shares.

Ajax. I'll knead him, I'll make him supple.

220 (*Nestor.* He's not yet through warm. Force him with praises: pour in, pour in; his ambition is dry.

Ulysses [*to Agamemnon*]. My lord, you feed too much on this dislike.

Nestor. Our noble general, do not do so.

Diomedes. You must prepare to fight without Achilles.

Ulysses. Why, 'tis this naming of him does him harm. Here is a man—but 'tis before his face: I will be silent.

Nestor.   Wherefore should you so? He is not emulous, as Achilles is.

Ulysses. Know the whole world, he is as valiant.

230 *Ajax.* A whoreson dog, that shall palter thus with us!
Would he were a Trojan!

Nestor. What a vice were it in Ajax now—

Ulysses. If he were proud—

Diomedes. Or covetous of praise—

Ulysses. Ay, or surly borne—

Diomedes. Or strange, or self-affected!

Ulysses. Thank the heavens, lord, thou art of sweet composure;
Praise him that got thee, she that gave thee suck;
Famed be thy tutor, and thy parts of nature

240 Thrice-famed beyond, beyond all erudition:
But he that disciplined thine arms to fight,

Let Mars divide eternity in twain,
And give him half; and, for thy vigour,
Bull-bearing Milo his addition yield
To sinewy Ajax. I will not praise thy wisdom,
Which, like a bourn, a pale, a shore, confines
Thy spacious and dilated parts. Here's Nestor,
Instructed by the antiquary times;
He must, he is, he cannot but be wise:
But pardon, father Nestor, were your days   250
As green as Ajax', and your brain so tempered,
You should not have the eminence of him,
But be as Ajax.
 Ajax.   Shall I call you father?
 Nestor. Ay, my good son.
 Diomedes.   Be ruled by him, Lord Ajax.
 Ulysses. There is no tarrying here: the
  hart Achilles
Keeps thicket. Please it our great general
To call together all his state of war:
Fresh kings are come to Troy; tomorrow
We must with all our main of power stand fast;
And here's a lord, come knights from east to west,   260
And cull their flower, Ajax shall cope the best.
 Agamemnon. Go we to council. Let Achilles sleep:
Light boats sail swift, though greater hulks draw deep.
           [they go

[3. 1.]   *Troy. Priam's palace*

   Enter PANDARUS *and a Servant*

 Pandarus. Friend, you, pray you, a word: do you not
follow the young Lord Paris?
 Servant. Ay sir, when he goes before me.

Pandarus. You depend upon him, I mean?

Servant. Sir, I do depend upon the Lord.

Pandarus. You depend upon a noble gentleman; I must needs praise him.

Servant. The Lord be praised!

Pandarus. You know me, do you not?

10 *Servant.* Faith, sir, superficially.

Pandarus. Friend, know me better: I am the Lord Pandarus.

Servant. I hope I shall know your honour better.

Pandarus. I do desire it.

Servant. You are in the state of grace.

Pandarus. Grace! not so, friend: honour and lordship are my titles. [*music within*] What music is this?

Servant. I do but partly know, sir: it is music in parts.

20 *Pandarus.* Know you the musicians?

Servant. Wholly, sir.

Pandarus. Who play they to?

Servant. To the hearers, sir.

Pandarus. At whose pleasure, friend?

Servant. At mine, sir, and theirs that love music.

Pandarus. Command, I mean, friend.

Servant. Who shall I command, sir?

Pandarus. Friend, we understand not one another: I am too courtly, and thou art too cunning. At whose
30 request do these men play?

Servant. That's to't, indeed, sir: marry, sir, at the request of Paris my lord, who is there in person; with him, the mortal Venus, the heart-blood of beauty, love's indivisible soul.

Pandarus. Who, my cousin Cressida?

Servant. No, sir, Helen. Could you not find out that by her attributes?

Pandarus. It should seem, fellow, that thou hast not seen the Lady Cressida. I come to speak with Paris from the Prince Troilus; I will make a complimental 40 assault upon him, for my business seethes.

(*Servant.* Sodden business! There's a stewed phrase indeed!

Enter PARIS and HELEN, attended

Pandarus. Fair be to you, my lord, and to all this fair company! Fair desires, in all fair measure, fairly guide them! Especially to you, fair queen, fair thoughts be your fair pillow!

Helen. Dear lord, you are full of fair words.

Pandarus. You speak your fair pleasure, sweet queen. Fair prince, here is good broken music. 50

Paris. You have broke it, cousin; and, by my life, you shall make it whole again: you shall piece it out with a piece of your performance. Nell, he is full of harmony.

Pandarus. Truly, lady, no.

Helen. O, sir—

Pandarus. Rude, in sooth; in good sooth, very rude.

Paris. Well said, my lord! well, you say so in fits.

Pandarus. I have business to my lord, dear queen. My lord, will you vouchsafe me a word? 60

Helen. Nay, this shall not hedge us out; we'll hear you sing, certainly.

Pandarus. Well, sweet queen, you are pleasant with me.—But, marry, thus, my lord: my dear lord, and most esteemed friend, your brother Troilus—

Helen. My Lord Pandarus; honey-sweet lord—

Pandarus. Go to, sweet queen, go to—commends himself most affectionately to you—

Helen. You shall not bob us out of our melody. If you do, our melancholy upon your head! 70

Pandarus. Sweet queen, sweet queen; that's a sweet queen, i'faith.

Helen. And to make a sweet lady sad is a sour offence.

Pandarus. Nay, that shall not serve your turn; that shall it not, in truth, la. Nay, I care not for such words; no, no.—And, my lord, he desires you, that if the king call for him at supper you will make his excuse.

Helen. My Lord Pandarus—

Pandarus. What says my sweet queen, my very very 80 sweet queen?

Paris. What exploit's in hand? where sups he tonight?

Helen. Nay, but, my lord—

Pandarus. What says my sweet queen?—My cousin will fall out with you. You must not know where he sups.

Paris. I'll lay my life, with my disposer Cressida.

Pandarus. No, no, no such matter; you are wide: come, your disposer is sick.

90 *Paris.* Well, I'll make's excuse.

Pandarus. Ay, good my lord. Why should you say Cressida? no, your poor disposer's sick.

Paris. I spy.

Pandarus. You spy! What do you spy? Come, give me an instrument. Now, sweet queen.

Helen. Why, this is kindly done.

Pandarus. My niece is horribly in love with a thing you have, sweet queen.

Helen. She shall have it, my lord, if it be not my 100 lord Paris.

Pandarus. He! no, she'll none of him; they two are twain.

Helen. Falling in, after falling out, may make them three.

Pandarus. Come, come, I'll hear no more of this. I'll sing you a song now.

Helen. Ay, ay, prithee now. By my troth, sweet lord, thou hast a fine forehead.

Pandarus. Ay, you may, you may.

Helen. Let thy song be love; this love will undo us all. 110 O Cupid, Cupid, Cupid!

Pandarus. Love! ay, that it shall, i'faith.

Paris. Ay, good now, love, love, nothing but love.

Pandarus. In good troth, it begins so.   [*sings*

Love, love, nothing but love, still love, still more!
     For, O, love's bow
     Shoots buck and doe;
     The shaft confounds
     Not that it wounds,
But tickles still the sore.   120
These lovers cry Oh, oh, they die!
     Yet that which seems the wound to kill,
Doth turn oh! oh! to ha! ha! he!
     So dying love lives still.
Oh! oh! a while, but ha! ha! ha!
Oh! oh! groans out for ha! ha! ha!

Heigh-ho!

Helen. In love, i'faith, to the very tip of the nose.

Paris. He eats nothing but doves, love, and that breeds hot blood, and hot blood begets hot thoughts, 130 and hot thoughts beget hot deeds, and hot deeds is love.

Pandarus. Is this the generation of love?—hot blood, hot thoughts, and hot deeds? Why, they are vipers. Is love a generation of vipers? Sweet lord, who's afield today?

Paris. Hector, Deiphobus, Helenus, Antenor, and all the gallantry of Troy. I would fain have armed

today, but my Nell would not have it so. How chance
my brother Troilus went not?

140 *Helen.* He hangs the lip at something; you know all,
Lord Pandarus.

Pandarus. Not I, honey-sweet queen. I long to hear
how they sped today.—You'll remember your brother's
excuse?

Paris. To a hair.

Pandarus. Farewell, sweet queen.

Helen. Commend me to your niece.

Pandarus. I will, sweet queen.   [*goes*
                                        [*retreat sounded*

Paris. They're come from th'field: let us to
            Priam's hall,

150 To greet the warriors. Sweet Helen, I must woo you
To help unarm our Hector. His stubborn buckles,
With these your white enchanting fingers touched,
Shall more obey than to the edge of steel
Or force of Greekish sinews. You shall do more
Than all the island kings—disarm great Hector.

Helen. 'Twill make us proud to be his
            servant, Paris;
Yea, what he shall receive of us in duty
Gives us more palm in beauty than we have,
Yea, overshines ourself.

160 *Paris.* Sweet, above thought I love thee.   [*they go*

[3. 2.]   *The same. Pandarus' orchard*

        Enter PANDARUS *and Troilus' Boy, meeting*

Pandarus. How now! Where's thy master? At my
cousin Cressida's?

Boy. No, sir; he stays for you to conduct him thither.
Pandarus. O, here he comes.

Enter TROILUS

How now, how now!
  Troilus. Sirrah, walk off.   [*Boy goes*
  Pandarus. Have you seen my cousin?
  Troilus. No, Pandarus; I stalk about her door,
Like a strange soul upon the Stygian banks
Staying for waftage. O, be thou my Charon,   10
And give me swift transportance to those fields
Where I may wallow in the lily beds
Proposed for the deserver!·O gentle Pandar,
From Cupid's shoulder pluck his painted wings,
And fly with me to Cressid!
  Pandarus. Walk here i'th'orchard; I'll bring her
straight.   [*goes*
  Troilus. I am giddy: expectation whirls me round.
Th'imaginary relish is so sweet
That it enchants my sense. What will it be   20
When that the watery palate tastes indeed
Love's thrice repuréd nectar?—death, I fear me,
Swooning distraction, or some joy too fine,
Too subtle-potent, tuned too sharp in sweetness,
For the capacity of my ruder powers;
I fear it much, and I do fear besides
That I shall lose distinction in my joys,
As doth a battle, when they charge on heaps
The enemy flying.

Re-enter PANDARUS

  Pandarus. She's making her ready; she'll come 30
straight. You must be witty now: she does so blush,
and fetches her wind so short as if she were frayed with

a sprite. I'll fetch her. It is the prettiest villain; she
fetches her breath as short as a new-ta'en sparrow.
                                                    [goes
    Troilus. Even such a passion doth embrace my bosom:
My heart beats thicker than a feverous pulse;
And all my powers do their bestowing lose,
Like vassalage at unawares encountering
The eye of majesty.

Re-enter PANDARUS *and* CRESSIDA

40   *Pandarus.* Come, come, what need you blush?
Shame's a baby. Here she is now. Swear the oaths
now to her that you have sworn to me. What, are you
gone again? You must be watched ere you be made tame,
must you? Come your ways, come your ways; an you
draw backward, we'll put you i'th' fills. Why do you not
speak to her? Come, draw this curtain, and let's see
your picture. Alas the day, how loath you are to offend
daylight! An 'twere dark, you'ld close sooner. So, so;
rub on, and kiss the mistress. How now! a kiss in fee-
50   farm!—build there, carpenter; the air is sweet. Nay,
you shall fight your hearts out ere I part you—the falcon
as the tercel, for all the ducks i'th'river. Go to, go to.
    Troilus. You have bereft me of all words, lady.
    Pandarus. Words pay no debts, give her deeds; but
she'll bereave you o'th'deeds too, if she call your
activity in question. What, billing again? Here's 'In
witness whereof the parties interchangeably'—Come in,
come in; I'll go get a fire.   [goes
    Cressida. Will you walk in, my lord?
60   *Troilus.* O Cressida, how often have I wished me
thus!
    Cressida. Wished, my lord?—The gods grant—O,
my lord!

Troilus. What should they grant? What makes this
pretty abruption? What too curious dreg espies my
sweet lady in the fountain of our love?

Cressida. More dregs than water, if my fears have eyes.

Troilus. Fears make devils of cherubins; they never
see truly.

Cressida. Blind fear, that seeing reason leads, finds 70
safer footing than blind reason stumbling without fear:
to fear the worst oft cures the worse.

Troilus. O, let my lady apprehend no fear: in all
Cupid's pageant there is presented no monster.

Cressida. Nor nothing monstrous neither?

Troilus. Nothing but our undertakings, when we vow
to weep seas, live in fire, eat rocks, tame tigers; thinking
it harder for our mistress to devise imposition enough
than for us to undergo any difficulty imposed. This is
the monstruosity in love, lady—that the will is infinite 80
and the execution confined; that the desire is boundless
and the act a slave to limit.

Cressida. They say all lovers swear more performance
than they are able, and yet reserve an ability that they
never perform; vowing more than the perfection of ten,
and discharging less than the tenth part of one. They
that have the voice of lions and the act of hares, are
they not monsters?

Troilus. Are there such? Such are not we. Praise us
as we are tasted, allow us as we prove. Our head shall 90
go bare till merit crown it: no perfection in reversion
shall have a praise in present. We will not name desert
before his birth; and, being born, his addition shall be
humble. Few words to fair faith: Troilus shall be such
to Cressid as what envy can say worst shall be a mock
for his truth; and what truth can speak truest, not truer
than Troilus.

Cressida. Will you walk in, my lord?

Re-enter PANDARUS

Pandarus. What, blushing still? Have you not done
100 talking yet?

Cressida. Well, uncle, what folly I commit, I dedicate
to you.

Pandarus. I thank you for that: if my lord get a boy
of you, you'll give him me. Be true to my lord; if he
flinch, chide me for it.

Troilus. You know now your hostages: your uncle's
word and my firm faith.

Pandarus. Nay, I'll give my word for her too. Our
kindred, though they be long ere they are wooed, they
110 are constant being won. They are burs, I can tell you;
they'll stick where they are thrown.

Cressida. Boldness comes to me now and brings
    me heart:
Prince Troilus, I have loved you night and day
For many weary months.

Troilus. Why was my Cressid then so hard to win?

Cressida. Hard to seem won; but I was won,
    my lord,
With the first glance that ever—pardon me;
If I confess much, you will play the tyrant.
I love you now; but not, till now, so much
120 But I might master it. In faith, I lie!
My thoughts were like unbridled children, grown
Too headstrong for their mother. See, we fools!
Why have I blabbed? Who shall be true to us,
When we are so unsecret to ourselves?
But, though I loved you well, I wooed you not;
And yet, good faith, I wished myself a man,
Or that we women had men's privilege

Of speaking first. Sweet, bid me hold my tongue;
For in this rapture I shall surely speak
The thing I shall repent. See, see, your silence,   130
Cunning in dumbness, from my weakness draws
My very soul of counsel! Stop my mouth.

   Troilus. And shall, albeit sweet music issues thence.
                                          [*kisses her*

   Pandarus. Pretty, i'faith.

   Cressida. My lord, I do beseech you, pardon me:
'Twas not my purpose thus to beg a kiss.
I am ashamed. O heavens! what have I done?
For this time will I take my leave, my lord.

   Troilus. Your leave, sweet Cressid?

   Pandarus. Leave! An you take leave till tomorrow   140
morning—

   Cressida. Pray you, content you.

   Troilus. What offends you, lady?

   Cressida. Sir, mine own company.

   Troilus. You cannot shun yourself.

   Cressida. Let me go and try.
I have a kind of self resides with you,
But an unkind self that itself will leave
To be another's fool. I would be gone.
Where is my wit? I know not what I speak.   150

   Troilus. Well know they what they speak that speak
       so wisely.

   Cressida. Perchance, my lord, I show more craft
       than love,
And fell so roundly to a large confession
To angle for your thoughts; but you are wise,
Or else you love not: for to be wise and love
Exceeds man's might; that dwells with gods above.

   Troilus. O that I thought it could be in a woman—
As, if it can, I will presume in you—

To feed for aye her lamp and flame of love;
160 To keep her constancy in plight and youth,
Outliving beauties outward, with a mind
That doth renew swifter than blood decays!
Or that persuasion could but thus convince me
That my integrity and truth to you
Might be affronted with the match and weight
Of such a winnowed purity in love—
How were I then uplifted! But, alas,
I am as true as truth's simplicity,
And simpler than the infancy of truth!
170 *Cressida.* In that I'll war with you.
　　Troilus.　　　　　　　　　O virtuous fight,
When right with right wars who shall be most right!
True swains in love shall in the world to come
Approve their truths by Troilus. When their rhymes,
Full of protest, of oath, and big compare,
Want similes, truth tired with iteration—
'As true as steel, as plantage to the moon,
As sun to day, as turtle to her mate,
As iron to adamant, as earth to th'centre'—
Yet, after all comparisons of truth,
180 As truth's authentic author to be cited,
'As true as Troilus' shall crown up the verse
And sanctify the numbers.
　　Cressida.　　　　　Prophet may you be!
If I be false, or swerve a hair from truth,
When time is old and hath forgot itself,
When waterdrops have worn the stones of Troy,
And blind oblivion swallowed cities up,
And mighty states characterless are grated
To dusty nothing, yet let memory,
From false to false, among false maids in love,
190 ·Upbraid my falsehood! When they've said 'as false

As air, as water, wind or sandy earth,
As fox to lamb, or wolf to heifer's calf,
Pard to the hind, or stepdame to her son',
Yea let them say, to stick the heart of falsehood,
'As false as Cressid'.

Pandarus. Go to, a bargain made. Seal it, seal it.
I'll be the witness. Here I hold your hand; here my
cousin's. If ever you prove false one to another, since
I have taken such pains to bring you together, let all
pitiful goers-between be called to the world's end after 200
my name—call them all Pandars: let all constant men
be Troiluses, all false women Cressids, and all brokers-
between Pandars! Say 'amen'.

Troilus. Amen.

Cressida. Amen.

Pandarus. Amen. Whereupon I will show you a
chamber with a bed; which bed, because it shall not
speak of your pretty encounters, press it to death. Away!

[*they go*

And Cupid grant all tongue-tied maidens here
Bed, chamber, pandar, to provide this gear!   [*goes* 210

[3. 3.]   *The Greek camp*

*Flourish. Enter AGAMEMNON, ULYSSES, DIOMEDES,
NESTOR, AJAX, MENELAUS, and CALCHAS*

Calchas. Now, princes, for the service I have done,
Th'advantage of the time prompts me aloud
To call for recompense. Appear it to your minds
That, through the sight I bear in things to come,
I have abandoned Troy, left my possession,
Incurred a traitor's name, exposed myself,

5   PST&C

From certain and possessed conveniences,
To doubtful fortunes; sequestering from me all
That time, acquaintance, custom and condition
10 Made tame and most familiar to my nature;
And here, to do you service, am become
As new into the world, strange, unacquainted.
I do beseech you, as in way of taste,
To give me now a little benefit
Out of those many registered in promise,
Which, you say, live to come in my behalf.
  Agamemnon. What wouldst thou of us, Trojan?
    Make demand.
  Calchas. You have a Trojan prisoner
    called Antenor,
Yesterday took; Troy holds him very dear.
20 Oft have you—often have you thanks therefore—
Desired my Cressid in right great exchange,
Whom Troy hath still denied; but this Antenor
I know is such a wrest in their affairs
That their negotiations all must slack,
Wanting his manage; and they will almost
Give us a prince of blood, a son of Priam,
In change of him. Let him be sent, great princes,
And he shall buy my daughter; and her presence
Shall quite strike off all service I have done
30 In most accepted pain.
  Agamemnon.   Let Diomed bear him,
And bring us Cressid hither; Calchas shall have
What he requests of us. Good Diomed,
Furnish you fairly for this interchange;
Withal, bring word if Hector will tomorrow
Be answered in his challenge: Ajax is ready.
  Diomedes. This shall I undertake, and 'tis a burden
Which I am proud to bear. [*Diomedes and Calchas go*

Enter ACHILLES and PATROCLUS, before their tent

Ulysses. Achilles stands i'th'entrance of his tent:
Please it our general pass strangely by him,
As if he were forgot; and, princes all, 40
Lay negligent and loose regard upon him.
I will come last. 'Tis like he'll question me
Why such unplausive eyes are bent on him.
If so, I have derision medicinable
To use between your strangeness and his pride,
Which his own will shall have desire to drink.
It may do good: pride hath no other glass
To show itself but pride; for supple knees
Feed arrogance and are the proud man's fees.
Agamemnon. We'll execute your purpose and put on 50
A form of strangeness as we pass along;
So do each lord, and either greet him not
Or else disdainfully, which shall shake him more
Than if not looked on. I will lead the way.
 [they pass along
Achilles. What, comes the general to speak with me?
You know my mind: I'll fight no more 'gainst Troy.
Agamemnon. What says Achilles? Would he aught
 with us?
Nestor. Would you, my lord, aught with the general?
Achilles. No.
Nestor. Nothing, my lord. 60
Agamemnon. The better. *[Agamemnon and Nestor go*
Achilles. Good day, good day.
Menelaus. How do you? how do you? *[goes*
Achilles. What, does the cuckold scorn me?
Ajax. How now, Patroclus!
Achilles. Good morrow, Ajax.
Ajax. Ha?

 5-2

Achilles. Good morrow.

Ajax. Ay, and good next day too.   [*goes*

70 *Achilles.* What mean these fellows? Know they
       not Achilles?

Patroclus. They pass by strangely. They were used
       to bend,

To send their smiles before them to Achilles,

To come as humbly as they use to creep

To holy altars.

Achilles.   What, am I poor of late?

'Tis certain, greatness, once fallen out with fortune,

Must fall out with men too. What the declined is

He shall as soon read in the eyes of others

As feel in his own fall; for men, like butterflies,

Show not their mealy wings but to the summer,

80 And not a man, for being simply man,

Hath any honour but honour for those honours

That are without him—as place, riches, and favour,

Prizes of accident as oft as merit;

Which, when they fall, as being slippery standers,

The love that leaned on them as slippery too,

Doth one pluck down another and together

Die in the fall. But 'tis not so with me:

Fortune and I are friends; I do enjoy

At ample point all that I did possess,

90 Save these men's looks; who do, methinks, find out

Something not worth in me such rich beholding

As they have often given. Here is Ulysses;

I'll interrupt his reading.

How now, Ulysses!

Ulysses.   Now, great Thetis' son!

Achilles. What are you reading?

Ulysses.   A strange fellow here

Writes me that man, how dearly ever parted,

How much in having, or without or in,
Cannot make boast to have that which he hath,
Nor feels not what he owes, but by reflection;
As when his virtues, shining upon others,   100
Heat them and they retort that heat again
To the first giver.

  Achilles.   This is not strange, Ulysses.
The beauty that is borne here in the face
The bearer knows not, but commends itself
To others' eyes; nor doth the eye itself,
That most pure spirit of sense, behold itself,
Not going from itself; but eye to eye opposed
Salutes each other with each other's form:
For speculation turns not to itself
Till it hath travelled and is mirrored there   110
Where it may see itself. This is not strange at all.

  Ulysses. I do not strain at the position—
It is familiar—but at the author's drift;
Who in his circumstance expressly proves
That no man is the lord of anything,
Though in and of him there be much consisting,
Till he communicate his parts to others;
Nor doth he of himself know them for aught
Till he behold them forméd in th'applause
Where they're extended; who, like an
    arch, reverberate   120
The voice again; or, like a gate of steel
Fronting the sun, receives and renders back
His figure and his heat. I was much rapt in this,
And apprehended here immediately
The unknown Ajax.
Heavens! what a man is there! a very horse,
That has he knows not what. Nature, what things
    there are

Most abject in regard and dear in use!
What things again most dear in the esteem
130 And poor in worth! Now shall we see tomorrow—
An act that very chance doth throw upon him—
Ajax renowned. O heavens, what some men do,
While some men leave to do!
How some men creep in skittish Fortune's hall,
Whiles others play the idiots in her eyes!
How one man eats into another's pride,
While pride is fasting in his wantonness!
To see these Grecian lords!—why, even already
They clap the lubber Ajax on the shoulder,
140 As if his foot were on brave Hector's breast
And great Troy shrinking.
  Achilles. I do believe it; for they passed by me
As misers do by beggars, neither gave to me
Good word nor look. What, are my deeds forgot?
  Ulysses. Time hath, my lord, a wallet at his back
Wherein he puts alms for oblivion,
A great-sized monster of ingratitude.
Those scraps are good deeds past, which are devoured
As fast as they are made, forgot as soon
150 As done. Perseverance, dear my lord,
Keeps honour bright: to have done, is to hang
Quite out of fashion, like a rusty mail
In monumental mockery. Take the instant way;
For honour travels in a strait so narrow
Where one but goes abreast. Keep then the path;
For emulation hath a thousand sons
That one by one pursue. If you give way,
Or hedge aside from the direct forthright,
Like to an entered tide they all rush by
160 And leave you hindmost;
Or, like a gallant horse fallen in first rank,

Lie there for pavement to the abject rear,
O'er-run and trampled on. Then what they do
    in present,
Though less than yours in past, must o'ertop yours;
For Time is like a fashionable host
That slightly shakes his parting guest by th'hand
And, with his arms outstretched as he would fly,
Grasps in the comer: welcome ever smiles,
And farewell goes out sighing. O, let not virtue seek
Remuneration for the thing it was;   170
For beauty, wit,
High birth, vigour of bone, desert in service,
Love, friendship, charity, are subject all
To envious and calumniating Time.
One touch of nature makes the whole world kin,
That all with one consent praise new-born gawds,
Though they are made and moulded of things past,
And give to dust that is a little gilt
More laud than gilt o'er-dusted.
The present eye praises the present object: 180
Then marvel not, thou great and complete man,
That all the Greeks begin to worship Ajax;
Since things in motion sooner catch the eye
Than what not stirs. The cry went once on thee,
And still it might, and yet it may again,
If thou wouldst not entomb thyself alive
And case thy reputation in thy tent,
Whose glorious deeds but in these fields of late
Made emulous missions 'mongst the gods themselves,
And drave great Mars to faction.
    Achilles.   Of this my privacy   190
I have strong reasons.
    Ulysses.   But 'gainst your privacy
The reasons are more potent and heroical.

'Tis known, Achilles, that you are in love
With one of Priam's daughters.

 Achilles.   Ha! known?
 Ulysses. Is that a wonder?
The providence that's in a watchful state
Knows almost every grain of Pluto's gold,
Finds bottom in th'uncomprehensive deeps,
Keeps place with thought and almost like the gods
200 Does thoughts unveil in their dumb cradles.
There is a mystery, with whom relation
Durst never meddle, in the soul of state,
Which hath an operation more divine
Than breath or pen can give expressure to.
All the commerce that you have had with Troy
As perfectly is ours as yours, my lord;
And better would it fit Achilles much
To throw down Hector than Polyxena.
But it must grieve young Pyrrhus now at home,
210 When fame shall in our islands sound her trump,
And all the Greekish girls shall tripping sing
'Great Hector's sister did Achilles win,
But our great Ajax bravely beat down him'.
Farewell, my lord. I as your lover speak:
The fool slides o'er the ice that you should break.

               [goes

 Patroclus. To this effect, Achilles, have I
  moved you.
A woman impudent and mannish grown
Is not more loathed than an effeminate man
In time of action. I stand condemned for this:
220 They think my little stomach to the war
And your great love to me restrains you thus.
Sweet, rouse yourself, and the weak wanton Cupid
Shall from your neck unloose his amorous fold

And, like a dew-drop from the lion's mane,
Be shook to air.
  Achilles.   Shall Ajax fight with Hector?
  Patroclus. Ay, and perhaps receive much honour
    by him.
  Achilles. I see my reputation is at stake;
My fame is shrewdly gored.
  Patroclus.   O, then, beware;
Those wounds heal ill that men do give themselves:
Omission to do what is necessary   230
Seals a commission to a blank of danger;
And danger, like an ague, subtly taints
Even then when we sit idly in the sun.
  Achilles. Go call Thersites hither, sweet Patroclus;
I'll send the fool to Ajax and desire him
T'invite the Trojan lords after the combat
To see us here unarmed. I have a woman's longing,
An appetite that I am sick withal,
To see great Hector in his weeds of peace,
To talk with him, and to behold his visage,   240
Even to my full of view.

Enter THERSITES

              A labour saved!
  Thersites. A wonder!
  Achilles. What?
  Thersites. Ajax goes up and down the field, asking
for himself.
  Achilles. How so?
  Thersites. He must fight singly tomorrow with Hector,
and is so prophetically proud of an heroical cudgelling
that he raves in saying nothing.
  Achilles. How can that be?   250
  Thersites. Why, 'a stalks up and down like a peacock—

a stride and a stand; ruminates like an hostess that hath
no arithmetic but her brain to set down her reckoning;
bites his lip with a politic regard, as who should say
'There were wit in this head, an 'twould out'—and so
there is; but it lies as coldly in him as fire in a flint,
which will not show without knocking. The man's
undone for ever, for if Hector break not his neck i'th'
combat, he'll break't himself in vainglory. He knows
260 not me. I said 'Good morrow, Ajax', and he replies
'Thanks, Agamemnon'. What think you of this man,
that takes me for the general? He's grown a very land-
fish, languageless, a monster. A plague of opinion!—
a man may wear it on both sides, like a leather jerkin.

Achilles. Thou must be my ambassador to him,
Thersites.

Thersites. Who, I? Why, he'll answer nobody. He
professes not answering. Speaking is for beggars; he
wears his tongue in's arms. I will put on his presence.
270 Let Patroclus make demands to me, you shall see the
pageant of Ajax.

Achilles. To him, Patroclus. Tell him I humbly
desire the valiant Ajax to invite the most valorous
Hector to come unarmed to my tent, and to procure
safe-conduct for his person of the magnanimous and
most illustrious six-or-seven-times-honoured captain-
general of the Grecian army, Agamemnon, et cetera.
Do this.

Patroclus. Jove bless great Ajax!
280 *Thersites.* Hum!

Patroclus. I come from the worthy Achilles—
Thersites. Ha!

Patroclus. Who most humbly desires you to invite
Hector to his tent—
Thersites. Hum!

Patroclus. And to procure safe-conduct from
Agamemnon.

Thersites. Agamemnon?

Patroclus. Ay, my lord.

Thersites. Ha! 290

Patroclus. What say you to't?

Thersites. God bu'y you, with all my heart.

Patroclus. Your answer, sir.

Thersites. If tomorrow be a fair day, by eleven o'clock
it will go one way or other. Howsoever, he shall pay
for me ere he has me.

Patroclus. Your answer, sir.

Thersites. Fare you well, with all my heart.

Achilles. Why, but he is not in this tune, is he?

Thersites. No, but he's out o' tune thus. What music 300
will be in him when Hector has knocked out his brains,
I know not; but, I am sure, none, unless the fiddler
Apollo get his sinews to make catlings on.

Achilles. Come, thou shalt bear a letter to him
straight.

Thersites. Let me carry another to his horse; for that's
the more capable creature.

Achilles. My mind is troubled like a fountain stirred,
And I myself see not the bottom of it.

[Achilles and Patroclus go in

Thersites. Would the fountain of your mind were 310
clear again, that I might water an ass at it! I had rather
be a tick in a sheep than such a valiant ignorance.

[goes

[4. 1.]   *Troy. A street*

Enter, at one side, ÆNEAS, and Servant with a torch; at the other, PARIS, DEIPHOBUS, ANTENOR, DIOMEDES, and others, with torches

   Paris. See, ho! who is that there?
   Deiphobus. It is the Lord Æneas.
   Æneas. Is the prince there in person?
Had I so good occasion to lie long
As you, Prince Paris, nothing but heavenly business
Should rob my bed-mate of my company.
   Diomedes. That's my mind too. Good morrow,
     Lord Æneas.
   Paris. A valiant Greek, Æneas—take his hand—
Witness the process of your speech, wherein
10 You told how Diomed, a whole week by days,
Did haunt you in the field.
   Æneas. Health to you, valiant sir,
During all question of the gentle truce;
But when I meet you armed, as black defiance
As heart can think or courage execute.
   Diomedes. The one and other Diomed embraces
Our bloods are now in calm; and so long, health!
But when contention and occasion meet,
By Jove, I'll play the hunter for thy life
20 With all my force, pursuit, and policy.
   Æneas. And thou shalt hunt a lion, that will fly
With his face backward. In humane gentleness,
Welcome to Troy! now, by Anchises' life,
Welcome indeed! By Venus' hand I swear
No man alive can love in such a sort
The thing he means to kill more excellently.
   Diomedes. We sympathise. Jove, let Æneas live,

If to my sword his fate be not the glory,
A thousand complete courses of the sun!
But, in mine emulous honour, let him die   30
With every joint a wound, and that tomorrow.
Æneas. We know each other well.
  Diomedes. We do; and long to know each other worse.
  Paris. This is the most despiteful-gentle greeting,
The noblest-hateful love, that e'er I heard of.
What business, lord, so early?
  Æneas. I was sent for to the king; but why,
      I know not.
  Paris. His purpose meets you: 'twas to bring this Greek
To Calchas' house, and there to render him,
For the enfreed Antenor, the fair Cressid.   40
Let's have your company, or, if you please,
Haste there before us. [aside] I constantly do think—
Or rather, call my thought a certain knowledge—
My brother Troilus lodges there tonight;
Rouse him and give him note of our approach,
With the whole quality wherefore; I fear
We shall be much unwelcome.
  (Æneas.   That I assure you;
Troilus had rather Troy were borne to Greece
Than Cressid borne from Troy.
  (Paris.   There is no help;
The bitter disposition of the time   50
Will have it so. [aloud] On, lord; we'll follow you.
  Æneas. Good morrow all.   [goes, with Servant
  Paris. And tell me, noble Diomed, faith, tell me true,
Even in the soul of sound good-fellowship,
Who, in your thoughts, merits fair Helen most,
Myself or Menelaus?
  Diomedes.   Both alike:
He merits well to have her that doth seek her,

Not making any scruple of her soilure,
With such a hell of pain and world of charge;
60 And you as well to keep her that defend her,
Not palating the taste of her dishonour,
With such a costly loss of wealth and friends.
He, like a puling cuckold, would drink up
The lees and dregs of a flat taméd piece;
You, like a lecher, out of whorish loins
Are pleased to breed out your inheritors.
Both merits poised, each weighs nor less nor more;
But he as he, the heavier for a whore.
    Paris. You are too bitter to your countrywoman.
70 *Diomedes.* She's bitter to her country. Hear me, Paris:
For every false drop in her bawdy veins
A Grecian's life hath sunk; for every scruple
Of her contaminated carrion weight
A Trojan hath been slain; since she could speak,
She hath not given so many good words breath
As for her Greeks and Trojans suffered death.
    Paris. Fair Diomed, you do as chapmen do,
Dispraise the thing that you desire to buy;
But we in silence hold this virtue well,
80 We'll but commend what we intend to sell.
Here lies our way.   [*they go*

[4. 2.] *The same. The court of Pandarus' house*

Enter TROILUS *and* CRESSIDA

    Troilus. Dear, trouble not yourself; the morn is cold.
    Cressida. Then, sweet my lord, I'll call mine
        uncle down;
He shall unbolt the gates.

Troilus.   Trouble him not;
To bed, to bed! sleep lull those pretty eyes,
And give as soft attachment to thy senses
As infants empty of all thought!
  Cressida.   Good morrow, then.
  Troilus. I prithee now, to bed!
  Cressida.   Are you aweary of me?
  Troilus. O Cressida! but that the busy day,
Waked by the lark, hath roused the ribald crows,
And dreaming night will hide our joys no longer,   10
I would not from thee.
  Cressida.   Night hath been too brief.
  Troilus. Beshrew the witch! with venomous wights
    she stays
As tediously as hell, but flies the grasps of love
With wings more momentary-swift than thought.
You will catch cold, and curse me.
  Cressida.   Prithee, tarry.
You men will never tarry.
O foolish Cressid! I might have still held off,
And then you would have tarried. Hark! there's
    one up.
  Pandarus [within]. What's all the doors open here?
  Troilus. It is your uncle.   20
  Cressida. A pestilence on him! now will he
    be mocking;
I shall have such a life!

Enter PANDARUS

  Pandarus. How now, how now! how go maiden-
heads? Here, you maid! where's my cousin Cressid?
  Cressida. Go hang yourself, you naughty
    mocking uncle!
You bring me to do—and then you flout me too.

Pandarus. To do what? to do what? let her say what!
What have I brought you to do?

    Cressida. Come, come, beshrew your heart! you'll
      ne'er be good,
30 Nor suffer others.

    Pandarus. Ha, ha! Alas, poor wretch! a poor
capocchia! Has't not slept tonight? Would he not,
a naughty man, let it sleep? A bugbear take him!

    Cressida. Did not I tell you? Would he were
      knocked i'th' head!   [*knocking*
Who's that at door? Good uncle, go and see.
My lord, come you again into my chamber.
You smile and mock me, as if I meant naughtily.

    Troilus. Ha, ha!

    Cressida. Come, you're deceived, I think of no
      such thing.   .   [*knocking*
40 How earnestly they knock! Pray you, come in;
I would not for half Troy have you seen here.

              [*Troilus and Cressida go in*

    Pandarus. Who's there? what's the matter? will you
beat down the door? How now! what's the matter?

Enter ÆNEAS

    Æneas. Good morrow, lord, good morrow.

    Pandarus. Who's there? my Lord Æneas! By my
troth, I knew you not. What news with you so early?

    Æneas. Is not prince Troilus here?

    Pandarus. Here! what should he do here?

    Æneas. Come, he is here, my lord. Do not
      deny him;
50 It doth import him much to speak with me.

    Pandarus. Is he here, say you? 'Tis more than I know,
I'll be sworn; for my own part, I came in late. What
should he do here?

Æneas. Ho! nay, then; come, come, you'll do him
wrong ere you're ware; you'll be so true to him, to be
false to him. Do not you know of him, but yet go fetch
him hither; go.   *Re-enter* TROILUS

Troilus. How now! what's the matter?
Æneas. My lord, I scarce have leisure to salute you,
My matter is so rash: there is at hand   60
Paris your brother and Deiphobus,
The Grecian Diomed, and our Antenor
Delivered to us; and for him forthwith,
Ere the first sacrifice, within this hour,
We must give up to Diomedes' hand
The Lady Cressida.
Troilus.   Is it so concluded?
Æneas. By Priam and the general state of Troy.
They are at hand and ready to effect it.
Troilus. How my achievements mock me!
I will go meet them; and, my Lord Æneas,   70
We met by chance: you did not find me here.
Æneas. Good, good, my lord; the secrets of
        neighbour Pandar
Have not more gift in taciturnity.
                        [*Troilus and Æneas go*
Pandarus. Is't possible? no sooner got but lost? The
devil take Antenor! The young prince will go mad.
A plague upon Antenor! I would they had broke's neck!

                Re-enter CRESSIDA

Cressida. How now! what's the matter? who was
here?
Pandarus. Ah, ah!
Cressida. Why sigh you so profoundly? Where's my   80
lord? Gone? Tell me, sweet uncle, what's the matter?

6

Pandarus. Would I were as deep under the earth as
I am above!

Cressida. O the gods! What's the matter?

Pandarus. Prithee, get thee in. Would thou hadst
ne'er been born! I knew thou wouldst be his death.
O, poor gentleman! A plague upon Antenor!

Cressida. Good uncle, I beseech you, on my knees
I beseech you, what's the matter?

90   *Pandarus.* Thou must be gone, wench, thou must be
gone; thou art changed for Antenor; thou must to thy
father, and be gone from Troilus: 'twill be his death;
'twill be his bane; he cannot bear it.

Cressida. O you immortal gods! I will not go.

Pandarus. Thou must.

Cressida. I will not, uncle. I have forgot my father;
I know no touch of consanguinity;
No kin, no love, no blood, no soul so near me
As the sweet Troilus. O you gods divine!
100   Make Cressid's name the very crown of falsehood,
If ever she leave Troilus! Time, force, and death,
Do to this body what extremes you can;
But the strong base and building of my love
Is as the very centre of the earth,
Drawing all things to it. I'll go in and weep——

Pandarus. Do, do.

Cressida. Tear my bright hair and scratch my
    praiséd cheeks,
Crack my clear voice with sobs and break my heart
With sounding Troilus. I will not go from Troy.

[*they go*

[4. 3.]   *The same. A street before Pandarus' house*

Enter PARIS, TROILUS, *followed by* ÆNEAS,
DEIPHOBUS, ANTENOR, *and* DIOMEDES

Paris. It is great morning, and the hour prefixed
For her delivery to this valiant Greek
Comes fast upon us. Good my brother Troilus,
Tell you the lady what she is to do
And haste her to the purpose.
  Troilus.   Walk into her house;
I'll bring her to the Grecian presently;
And to his hand when I deliver her,
Think it an altar, and thy brother Troilus
A priest, there offering to it his own heart.   [*goes*
  Paris. I know what 'tis to love,   10
And would, as I shall pity, I could help!
Please you walk in, my lords.   [*they go*

[4. 4.]   *The same. Pandarus' house*

Enter PANDARUS *and* CRESSIDA

Pandarus. Be moderate, be moderate.
  Cressida. Why tell you me of moderation?
The grief is fine, full, perfect, that I taste,
And violenteth in a sense as strong
As that which causeth it. How can I moderate it?
If I could temporise with my affection,
Or brew it to a weak and colder palate,
The like allayment could I give my grief.
My love admits no qualifying dross;
No more my grief, in such a precious loss.   10

6-2

Enter TROILUS

Pandarus. Here, here, here he comes. Ah sweet
ducks!

Cressida. O Troilus! Troilus!   [*embracing him*

Pandarus. What a pair of spectacles is here! Let me
embrace too. 'O heart', as the goodly saying is,

      O heart, O heavy heart,

      Why sigh'st thou without breaking?

where he answers again,

      Because thou canst not ease thy smart

20   By friendship nor by speaking.

There was never a truer rhyme. Let us cast away
nothing, for we may live to have need of such a verse.
We see it, we see it. How now, lambs!

Troilus. Cressid, I love thee in so strained a purity,
That the blest gods, as angry with my fancy,
More bright in zeal than the devotion which
Cold lips blow to their deities, take thee from me.

Cressida. Have the gods envy?

Pandarus. Ay, ay, ay, ay; 'tis too plain a case.

30 *Cressida.* And is it true that I must go from Troy?

Troilus. A hateful truth.

Cressida.   What, and from Troilus too?

Troilus. From Troy and Troilus.

Cressida.   Is it possible?

Troilus. And suddenly; where injury of chance
Puts back leave-taking, jostles roughly by
All time of pause, rudely beguiles our lips
Of all rejoindure, forcibly prevents
Our locked embraces, strangles our dear vows
Even in the birth of our own labouring breath.
We two, that with so many thousand sighs

40 Did buy each other, must poorly sell ourselves

With the rude brevity and discharge of one.
Injurious Time now with a robber's haste
Crams his rich thievery up, he knows not how:
As many farewells as be stars in heaven,
With distinct breath and consigned kisses to them,
He fumbles up into a loose adieu,
And scants us with a single famished kiss,
Distasted with the salt of broken tears.

Æneas [*within*]. My lord, is the lady ready?

Troilus. Hark! you are called. Some say the
    Genius so   50
Cries 'Come!' to him that instantly must die.
Bid them have patience; she shall come anon.

Pandarus. Where are my tears? Rain, to lay this wind,
or my heart will be blown up by th'root!   [*goes*

Cressida. I must then to the Grecians?

Troilus.   No remedy.

Cressida. A woeful Cressid 'mongst the
    merry Greeks!
When shall we see again?

Troilus. Hear me, my love: be thou but true
    of heart—

Cressida. I true! how now! what wicked deem
    is this?

Troilus. Nay, we must use expostulation kindly,   60
For it is parting from us.
I speak not 'be thou true', as fearing thee,
For I will throw my glove to Death himself
That there's no maculation in thy heart;
But 'be thou true' say I, to fashion in
My sequent protestation: be thou true,
And I will see thee.

Cressida. O, you shall be exposed, my lord, to dangers
As infinite as imminent! But I'll be true.

70 *Troilus.* And I'll grow friend with danger. Wear
        this sleeve.
      Cressida. And you this glove. When shall I see you?
      Troilus. I will corrupt the Grecian sentinels,
    To give thee nightly visitation.
    But yet, be true.
      Cressida.   O heavens! 'Be true' again!
      Troilus. Hear why I speak it, love:
    The Grecian youths are full of quality;
    Their loving well composed with gifts of nature,
    And flowing o'er with arts and exercise.
    How novelties may move and parts with person—
80 Alas, a kind of godly jealousy,
    Which, I beseech you, call a virtuous sin—
    Makes me afeard.
      Cressida.   O heavens! you love me not.
      Troilus. Die I a villain then!
    In this I do not call your faith in question
    So mainly as my-merit: I cannot sing,
    Nor heel the high lavolt, nor sweeten talk,
    Nor play at subtle games—fair virtues all,
    To which the Grecians are most prompt
        and pregnant;
    But I can tell that in each grace of these
90 There lurks a still and dumb-discoursive devil
    That tempts most cunningly. But be not tempted.
      Cressida. Do you think I will?
      Troilus. No;
    But something may be done that we will not,
    And sometimes we are devils to ourselves,
    When we will tempt the frailty of our powers,
    Presuming on their changeful potency.
      Æneas [within]. Nay, good my lord!
      Troilus.   Come, kiss; and let us part.

Paris [*within*]. Brother Troilus!
Troilus.   Good brother, come
     you hither;
And bring Æneas and the Grecian with you.   100
   Cressida. My lord, will you be true?
   Troilus. Who, I? alas, it is my vice, my fault!
Whiles others fish with craft for great opinion,
I with great truth catch mere simplicity;
Whilst some with cunning gild their copper crowns,
With truth and plainness I do wear mine bare.
Fear not my truth: the moral of my wit
Is 'plain and true'; there's all the reach of it.

     Enter ÆNEAS, PARIS, ANTENOR, DEIPHOBUS,
            and DIOMEDES

Welcome, Sir Diomed! Here is the lady
Which for Antenor we deliver you.   110
At the port, lord, I'll give her to thy hand,
And by the way possess thee what she is.
Entreat her fair; and, by my soul, fair Greek,
If e'er thou stand at mercy of my sword,
Name Cressid, and thy life shall be as safe
As Priam is in Ilion.
   Diomedes.   Fair Lady Cressid,
So please you, save the thanks this prince expects.
The lustre in your eye, heaven in your cheek,
Pleads your fair usage; and to Diomed
You shall be mistress, and command him wholly.   120
   Troilus. Grecian, thou dost not use me courteously,
To shame the zeal of my petition to thee
In praising her. I tell thee, lord of Greece,
She is as far high-soaring o'er thy praises
As thou unworthy to be called her servant.
I charge thee use her well, even for my charge;

For, by the dreadful Pluto, if thou dost not,
Though the great bulk Achilles be thy guard,
I'll cut thy throat.

 Diomedes.   O, be not moved, Prince Troilus.
130 Let me be privileged by my place and message
To be a speaker free. When I am hence,
I'll answer to my lust; and know you, lord,
I'll nothing do on charge: to her own worth
She shall be prized; but that you say 'Be't so',
I'll speak it in my spirit and honour 'No!'

 Troilus. Come, to the port. I'll tell thee, Diomed,
This brave shall oft make thee to hide thy head.
Lady, give me your hand; and, as we walk,
To our own selves bend we our needful talk.

      [Troilus, Cressida, and Diomedes go;
            trumpet sounds

140 *Paris.* Hark! Hector's trumpet.
 Æneas.   How have we spent
  this morning!
The prince must think me tardy and remiss,
That swore to ride before him to the field.

 Paris. 'Tis Troilus' fault; come, come, to field
  with him.

 Deiphobus. Let us make ready straight.

 Æneas. Yea, with a bridegroom's fresh alacrity,
Let us address to tend on Hector's heels.
The glory of our Troy doth this day lie
On his fair worth and single chivalry.   *[they go*

[4. 5.]　　　*The Greek camp. Lists set out*

*Enter AJAX, armed; AGAMEMNON, ACHILLES, PATRO-
CLUS, MENELAUS, ULYSSES, NESTOR, and others*

Agamemnon.　Here art thou in appointment fresh
　　and fair,
Anticipating time with starting courage.
Give with thy trumpet a loud note to Troy,
Thou dreadful Ajax, that the appalléd air
May pierce the head of the great combatant
And hale him hither.
　　Ajax.　　　　　　　Thou trumpet, there's my purse.
Now crack thy lungs, and split thy brazen pipe;
Blow, villain, till thy spheréd bias cheek
Outswell the choller of puffed Aquilon.
Come, stretch thy chest, and let thy eyes spout blood;　10
Thou blow'st for Hector.　　　　　　[*trumpet sounds*
　　Ulysses.　No trumpet answers.
　　Achilles.　　　　　　　'Tis but early days.
　　Agamemnon.　Is not yon Diomed, with
　　Calchas' daughter?
　　Ulysses.　'Tis he, I ken the manner of his gait:
He rises on the toe; that spirit of his
In aspiration lifts him from the earth.

Enter DIOMEDES, with CRESSIDA

　　Agamemnon.　Is this the Lady Cressid?
　　Diomedes.　　　　　　　Even she.
　　Agamemnon.　Most dearly welcome to the Greeks,
　　sweet lady.　　　　　　　　　[*kisses her*
　　Nestor.　Our general doth salute you with a kiss.
　　Ulysses.　Yet is the kindness but particular;　20
'Twere better she were kissed in general.

Nestor. And very courtly counsel. I'll begin.
So much for Nestor.   [*kisses her*
  Achilles. I'll take that winter from your lips,
    fair lady.
Achilles bids you welcome.   [*kisses her*
  Menelaus. I had good argument for kissing once.
  Patroclus. But that's no argument for kissing now;
For thus popped Paris in his hardiment,
And parted thus you and your argument. [*kisses her*
30   (*Ulysses.* O deadly gall, and theme of all our scorns!
For which we lose our heads to gild his horns.
  Patroclus. The first was Menelaus' kiss; this, mine—
Patroclus kisses you.   [*kisses her again*
  Menelaus.   O, this is trim!
  Patroclus. Paris and I kiss evermore for him.
  Menelaus. I'll have my kiss, sir. Lady, by your leave.
  Cressida. In kissing, do you render or receive?
  Menelaus. Both take and give.
  Cressida.   I'll make my match
    to live,
The kiss you take is better than you give;
Therefore no kiss.
40 *Menelaus.* I'll give you boot, I'll give you three
    for one.
  Cressida. You're an odd man; give even, or
    give none.
  Menelaus. An odd man, lady! every man is odd.
  Cressida. No, Paris is not; for you know 'tis true
That you are odd, and he is even with you.
  Menelaus. You fillip me o'th' head.
  Cressida.   No, I'll be sworn.
  Ulysses. It were no match, your nail against
    his horn.
May I, sweet lady, beg a kiss of you?

Cressida. You may.

Ulysses.   I do desire it.

Cressida.   Why, beg too.

Ulysses. Why then, for Venus' sake, give me a kiss
When Helen is a maid again, and his.   50

Cressida. I am your debtor; claim it when 'tis due.

Ulysses. Never's my day, and then a kiss of you.

Diomedes. Lady, a word; I'll bring you to
          your father.   [*goes, with Cressida*

Nestor. A woman of quick sense.

Ulysses.   Fie, fie upon her!
There's language in her eye, her cheek, her lip,
Nay, her foot speaks; her wanton spirits look out
At every joint and motive of her body.
O, these encounterers, so glib of tongue,
That give accosting welcome ere it comes,
And wide unclasp the tables of their thoughts   60
To every tickling reader!—set them down
For sluttish spoils of opportunity
And daughters of the game.   [*trumpet within*

All. The Trojans' trumpet.

Agamemnon.   Yonder comes the troop.

Flourish. Enter HECTOR, *armed;* ÆNEAS, TROILUS,
          and other Trojans, with Attendants

Æneas. Hail, all the state of Greece! What shall
          be done
To him that victory commands? Or do you purpose
A victor shall be known? Will you the knights
Shall to the edge of all extremity
Pursue each other, or shall they be divided
By any voice or order of the field?   70
Hector bade ask.

Agamemnon.   Which way would Hector have it?

Æneas. He cares not; he'll obey conditions.

Agamemnon. 'Tis done like Hector.

Achilles.   But securely done,
A little proudly, and great deal misprizing
The knight opposed.

Æneas.   If not Achilles, sir,
What is your name?

Achilles.   If not Achilles, nothing.

Æneas. Therefore Achilles. But whate'er, know this:
In the extremity of great and little,
Valour and pride excel themselves in Hector;
80 The one almost as infinite as all,
The other blank as nothing. Weigh him well,
And that which looks like pride is courtesy.
This Ajax is half made of Hector's blood;
In love whereof, half Hector stays at home;
Half heart, half hand, half Hector comes to seek
This blended knight, half Trojan and half Greek.

Achilles. A maiden battle then? O, I perceive you.

Re-enter DIOMEDES

Agamemnon. Here is Sir Diomed. Go,
     gentle knight,
Stand by our Ajax. As you and Lord Æneas
90 Consent upon the order of their fight,
So be it; either to the uttermost,
Or else a breath. The combatants being kin
Half stints their strife before their strokes begin.
               [*Ajax and Hector enter the lists*

Ulysses. They are opposed already.

Agamemnon. What Trojan is that same that looks
     so heavy?

Ulysses. The youngest son of Priam, a true knight;
Not yet mature, yet matchless-firm of word;

Speaking in deeds and deedless in his tongue;
Not soon provoked nor, being provoked, soon calmed;
His heart and hand both open and both free;   100
For what he has he gives, what thinks he shows;
Yet gives he not till judgement guide his bounty,
Nor dignifies an impair thought with breath;
Manly as Hector, but more dangerous;
For Hector in his blaze of wrath subscribes
To tender objects, but he in heat of action
Is more vindicative than jealous love;
They call him Troilus, and on him erect
A second hope, as fairly built as Hector:
Thus says Æneas, one that knows the youth   110
Even to his inches, and with private soul
Did in great Ilion thus translate him to me.
                    [alarum; Hector and Ajax fight

  Agamemnon. They are in action.
  Nestor. Now, Ajax, hold thine own!
  Troilus.   Hector, thou sleep'st;
Awake thee!
  Agamemnon. His blows are well disposed.
    There, Ajax!   *[trumpets cease*
  Diomedes. You must no more.
  Æneas.   Princes, enough, so please you.
  Ajax. I am not warm yet; let us fight again.
  Diomedes. As Hector pleases.
  Hector.   Why, then will I no more:
Thou art, great lord, my father's sister's son,   120
A cousin-german to great Priam's seed;
The obligation of our blood forbids
A gory emulation 'twixt us twain.
Were thy commixtion Greek and Trojan so,
That thou couldst say 'This hand is Grecian all,
And this is Trojan; the sinews of this leg

All Greek, and this all Troy; my mother's blood
Runs on the dexter cheek, and this sinister
Bounds in my father's', by Jove multipotent,
130 Thou shouldst not bear from me a Greekish member
Wherein my sword had not impressure made
Of our rank feud; but the just gods gainsay
That any drop thou borrow'dst from thy mother,
My sacred aunt, should by my mortal sword
Be drainéd! Let me embrace thee, Ajax.
By him that thunders, thou hast lusty arms;
Hector would have them fall upon him thus.
Cousin, all honour to thee!
    Ajax.   I thank thee, Hector.
Thou art too gentle and too free a man.
140 I came to kill thee, cousin, and bear hence
A great addition earnéd in thy death.
    Hector. Not Neoptolemus so mirable,
On whose bright crest Fame with her loud'st oyez
Cries 'This is he', could promise to himself
A thought of added honour torn from Hector.
    Æneas. There is expectance here from both
        the sides
What further you will do.
    Hector.   We'll answer it:
The issue is embracement; Ajax, farewell.
    Ajax. If I might in entreaties find success,
150 As seld I have the chance, I would desire
My famous cousin to our Grecian tents.
    Diomedes. 'Tis Agamemnon's wish; and
        great Achilles
Doth long to see unarmed the valiant Hector.
    Hector. Æneas, call my brother Troilus to me,
And signify this loving interview
To the expecters of our Trojan part;

Desire them home. Give me thy hand, my cousin;
I will go eat with thee, and see your knights.

 Ajax. Great Agamemnon comes to meet us here.

 Hector. The worthiest of them tell me name
  by name;   160
But for Achilles, my own searching eyes
Shall find him by his large and portly size.

 Agamemnon. Worthy of arms! as welcome as to one
That would be rid of such an enemy—
But that's no welcome; understand more clear,
What's past and what's to come is strewed with husks
And formless ruin of oblivion;
But in this extant moment, faith and troth,
Strained purely from all hollow bias-drawing,
Bids thee, with most divine integrity,   170
From heart of very heart, great Hector, welcome.

 Hector. I thank thee, most imperious Agamemnon.

 Agamemnon [*to Troilus*]. My well-famed lord of
  Troy, no less to you.

 Menelaus. Let me confirm my princely
  brother's greeting;
You brace of warlike brothers, welcome hither.

 Hector. Who must we answer?

 Æneas.   The noble Menelaus.

 Hector. O, you, my lord! by Mars his
  gauntlet, thanks!
Mock not that I affect th'untraded oath;
Your quondam wife swears still by Venus' glove.
She's well, but bade me not commend her to you. 180

 Menelaus. Name her not now, sir; she's a
  deadly theme.

 Hector. O, pardon; I offend.

 Nestor. I have, thou gallant Trojan, seen thee oft,
Labouring for destiny, make cruel way

Through ranks of Greekish youth; and I have
    seen thee,
As hot as Perseus, spur thy Phrygian steed,
And seen thee scorning forfeits and subduements
When thou hast hung thy advancéd sword i'th'air,
Not letting it decline on the declined,
190 That I have said to some my standers-by
'Lo, Jupiter is yonder, dealing life!'
And I have seen thee pause and take thy breath
When that a ring of Greeks have hemmed thee in,
Like an Olympian wrestling. This have I seen,
But this thy countenance, still locked in steel,
I never saw till now. I knew thy grandsire,
And once fought with him. He was a soldier good;
But, by great Mars the captain of us all,
Never like thee. O, let an old man embrace thee;
200 And, worthy warrior, welcome to our tents.
    Æneas. 'Tis the old Nestor.
    Hector. Let me embrace thee, good old chronicle,
That hast so long walked hand in hand with time;
Most reverend Nestor, I am glad to clasp thee.
    Nestor. I would my arms could match thee
    in contention,
As they contend with thee in courtesy.
    Hector. I would they could.
    Nestor. Ha!
By this white beard, I'ld fight with thee tomorrow.
210 Well, welcome, welcome! I have seen the time.
    Ulysses. I wonder now how yonder city stands
When we have here her base and pillar by us.
    Hector. I know your favour, Lord Ulysses, well.
Ah, sir, there's many a Greek and Trojan dead,
Since first I saw yourself and Diomed
In Ilion, on your Greekish embassy.

Ulysses. Sir, I foretold you then what would ensue.
My prophecy is but half his journey yet;
For yonder walls, that pertly front your town,
Yon towers, whose wanton tops do buss the clouds,   220
Must kiss their own feet.
  Hector.   I must not believe you.
There they stand yet; and modestly I think
The fall of every Phrygian stone will cost
A drop of Grecian blood. The end crowns all;
And that old common arbitrator, Time,
Will one day end it.
  Ulysses.   So to him we leave it.
Most gentle and most valiant Hector, welcome.
After the general, I beseech you next
To feast with me and see me at my tent.
  Achilles. I shall forestall thee, Lord Ulysses, thou!   230
Now Hector, I have fed mine eyes on thee;
I have with exact view perused thee, Hector,
And quoted joint by joint.
  Hector.   Is this Achilles?
  Achilles. I am Achilles.
  Hector. Stand fair, I pray thee; let me look on thee.
  Achilles. Behold thy fill.
  Hector.   Nay, I have done already.
  Achilles. Thou art too brief. I will the second time,
As I would buy thee, view thee limb by limb.
  Hector. O, like a book of sport thou'lt read me o'er;
But there's more in me than thou understand'st.   240
Why dost thou so oppress me with thine eye?
  Achilles. Tell me, you heavens, in which part of
     his body
Shall I destroy him?—whether there, or there,
     or there?—
That I may give the local wound a name,

  7

And make distinct the very breach whereout
Hector's great spirit flew. Answer me, heavens!
  Hector. It would discredit the blest gods, proud man,
To answer such a question. Stand again;
Think'st thou to catch my life so pleasantly
250 As to prenominate in nice conjecture
Where thou wilt hit me dead?
  Achilles.   I tell thee yea.
  Hector. Wert thou an oracle to tell me so,
I'ld not believe thee. Henceforth guard thee well;
For I'll not kill thee there, nor there, nor there;
But, by the forge that stithied Mars his helm,
I'll kill thee everywhere, yea, o'er and o'er.
You wisest Grecians, pardon me this brag:
His insolence draws folly from my lips;
But I'll endeavour deeds to match these words,
260 Or may I never—
  Ajax.   Do not chafe thee, cousin;
And you, Achilles, let these threats alone
Till accident or purpose bring you to't.
You may have every day enough of Hector,
If you have stomach. The general state, I fear,
Can scarce entreat you to be odd with him.
  Hector. I pray you, let us see you in the field;
We have had pelting wars since you refused
The Grecians' cause.
  Achilles.   Dost thou entreat me, Hector?
Tomorrow do I meet thee, fell as death;
270 Tonight all friends.
  Hector.   Thy hand upon that match.
  Agamemnon. First, all you peers of Greece, go to
    my tent;
There in the full convive we. Afterwards,
As Hector's leisure and your bounties shall

Concur together, severally entreat him.
Beat loud the taborins, let the trumpets blow,
That this great soldier may his welcome know.

       [Flourish; all go but Troilus and Ulysses

  Troilus. My Lord Ulysses, tell me, I beseech you,
In what place of the field doth Calchas keep?

  Ulysses. At Menelaus' tent, most princely Troilus.
There Diomed doth feast with him tonight;   280
Who neither looks upon the heaven nor earth,
But gives all gaze and bent of amorous view
On the fair Cressid.

  Troilus. Shall I, sweet lord, be bound to you
    so much,
After we part from Agamemnon's tent,
To bring me thither?

  Ulysses.   You shall command me, sir.
As gentle tell me, of what honour was
This Cressida in Troy? Had she no lover there
That wails her absence?

  Troilus. O, sir, to such as boasting show their scars, 290
A mock is due. Will you walk on, my lord?
She was beloved, she loved; she is, and doth;
But still sweet love is food for fortune's tooth.

                          [they go

[5. 1.]   *The same. Before Achilles' tent*

        Enter ACHILLES and PATROCLUS

  Achilles. I'll heat his blood with Greekish
    wine tonight,
Which with my scimitar I'll cool tomorrow.
Patroclus, let us feast him to the height.

  Patroclus. Here comes Thersites.

                           7-2

Enter THERSITES

Achilles.   How now, thou core of envy!
Thou crusty botch of nature, what's the news?

Thersites. Why, thou picture of what thou seemest,
and idol of idiot-worshippers, here's a letter for thee.

Achilles. From whence, fragment?

Thersites. Why, thou full dish of fool, from Troy.

10 *Patroclus.* Who keeps the tent now?

Thersites. The surgeon's box, or the patient's wound.

Patroclus. Well said, adversity! and what need these
tricks?

Thersites. Prithee, be silent, boy; I profit not by thy
talk; thou art thought to be Achilles' male varlet.

Patroclus. Male varlet, you rogue! what's that?

Thersites. Why, his masculine whore. Now, the rotten
diseases of the south, the guts-griping, ruptures, catarrhs,
loads o' gravel i'th'back, lethargies, cold palsies, raw
20 eyes, dirt-rotten livers, wheezing lungs, bladders full
of impostume, sciaticas, limekilns i'th'palm, incurable
bone-ache, and the rivelled fee-simple of the tetter,
take and take again such preposterous discoveries!

Patroclus. Why, thou damnable box of envy, thou;
what mean'st thou to curse thus?

Thersites. Do I curse thee?

Patroclus. Why, no, you ruinous butt; you whoreson
indistinguishable cur, no.

Thersites. No! Why art thou then exasperate, thou
30 idle immaterial skein of sleave-silk, thou green sarsenet
flap for a sore eye, thou tassel of a prodigal's purse,
thou? Ah, how the poor world is pestered with such
waterflies, diminutives of nature!

Patroclus. Out, gall!

Thersites. Finch-egg!

Achilles. My sweet Patroclus, I am thwarted quite
From my great purpose in tomorrow's battle.
Here is a letter from Queen Hecuba,
A token from her daughter, my fair love,
Both taxing me and gaging me to keep   40
An oath that I have sworn. I will not break it:
Fall Greeks; fail fame; honour or go or stay;
My major vow lies here; this I'll obey.
Come, come, Thersites, help to trim my tent;
This night in banqueting must all be spent.
Away, Patroclus!   [*Achilles and Patroclus go in*

Thersites. With too much blood and too little brain,
these two may run mad; but if with too much brain and
too little blood they do, I'll be a curer of madmen.
Here's Agamemnon, an honest fellow enough and one   50
that loves quails, but he has not so much brain as ear-
wax; and the goodly transformation of Jupiter there,
his brother, the bull, the primitive statue and oblique
memorial of cuckolds, a thrifty shoeing-horn in a chain,
hanging at his brother's leg—to what form but that he
is, should wit larded with malice and malice forced with
wit turn him to? To an ass, were nothing: he is both ass
and ox; to an ox, were nothing: he is both ox and ass.
To be a dog, a mule, a cat, a fitchew, a toad, a lizard,
an owl, a puttock, or a herring without a roe, I would   60
not care; but to be Menelaus, I would conspire against
destiny! Ask me not what I would be, if I were not
Thersites; for I care not to be the louse of a lazar, so
I were not Menelaus. Hoy-day! spirits and fires!

Enter HECTOR, TROILUS, A*J*AX, AGAMEMNON,
ULYSSES, NESTOR, MENELAUS, *and* DIOMEDES, *with
lights*

Agamemnon. We go wrong, we go wrong.

Ajax.   No, yonder 'tis;
There, where we see the lights.
Hector.   I trouble you.
Ajax. No, not a whit.

Re-enter ACHILLES

Ulysses.   Here comes himself to guide you.
Achilles. Welcome, brave Hector; welcome,
      princes all.
Agamemnon. So now, fair Prince of Troy, I bid
      good night.
70 Ajax commands the guard to tend on you.
Hector. Thanks and good night to the
      Greeks' general.
Menelaus. Good night, my lord.
Hector.   Good night, sweet Lord Menelaus.
(*Thersites.* Sweet draught: sweet, quoth 'a! sweet
sink, sweet sewer.
Achilles. Good night and welcome, both at once,
      to those
That go or tarry.
Agamemnon. Good night.
                              [*Agamemnon and Menelaus go*
Achilles. Old Nestor tarries; and you too, Diomed,
Keep Hector company an hour or two.
80 *Diomedes.* I cannot, lord; I have important business,
The tide whereof is now. Good night, great Hector.
Hector. Give me your hand.
Ulysses [*aside to Troilus*]. Follow his torch; he goes
      to Calchas' tent.
I'll keep you company.
Troilus.   Sweet sir, you honour me.
Hector. And so, good night.
                  [*Diomedes goes; Ulysses and Troilus following*

Achilles. Come, come, enter my tent.

            [*Achilles, Hector, Ajax and Nestor go in*

Thersites. That same Diomed's a false-hearted rogue,
a most unjust knave; I will no more trust him when he
leers than I will a serpent when he hisses; he will spend
his mouth and promise, like Babbler the hound; but
when he performs, astronomers foretell it; it is pro- 90
digious, there will come some change; the sun borrows
of the moon when Diomed keeps his word. I will
rather leave to see Hector than not to dog him. They
say he keeps a Trojan drab and uses the traitor Calchas'
tent; I'll after. Nothing but lechery! all incontinent
varlets!   [*goes*

[5. 2.]   *The same. Before Calchas' tent*

              Enter DIOMEDES

Diomedes. What, are you up here, ho? speak.
Calchas [*within*]. Who calls?
Diomedes. Diomed. Calchas, I think. Where's your
daughter?
Calchas [*within*]. She comes to you.

    Enter TROILUS *and* ULYSSES, *at a distance;*
           after them THERSITES

Ulysses. Stand where the torch may not discover us.

              Enter CRESSIDA

Troilus. Cressid comes forth to him.
Diomedes.   How now, my charge!
Cressida. Now, my sweet guardian! Hark, a word
    with you.   [*whispers*

Troilus. Yea, so familiar!

10   *Ulysses.* She will sing any man at first sight.

Thersites. And any man may sing her, if he can take her clef; she's noted.

Diomedes. Will you remember?

Cressida. Remember? Yes.

Diomedes. Nay, but do then;

And let your mind be coupled with your words.

Troilus. What should she remember?

Ulysses. List.

Cressida. Sweet honey Greek, tempt me no more
      to folly.

20   *Thersites.* Roguery!

Diomedes. Nay, then—

Cressida. I'll tell you what—

Diomedes. Foh, foh! come, tell a pin; you are forsworn.

Cressida. In faith, I cannot. What would you have
      me do?

Thersites. A juggling trick—to be secretly open.

Diomedes. What did you swear you would bestow
      on me?

Cressida. I prithee, do not hold me to mine oath;

Bid me do anything but that, sweet Greek.

Diomedes. Good night.

30   *Troilus.* Hold, patience!

Ulysses. How now, Trojan!

Cressida. Diomed—

Diomedes. No no, good night; I'll be your fool
      no more.

Troilus. Thy better must.

Cressida. Hark, one word in your ear.

Troilus. O plague and madness!

Ulysses. You are moved, prince; let us depart,
      I pray you,

Lest your displeasure should enlarge itself
To wrathful terms. This place is dangerous;
The time right deadly; I beseech you, go.   40
  Troilus. Behold, I pray you!
  Ulysses.   Nay, good my lord, go off;
You flow to great distraction; come, my lord.
  Troilus. I pray thee, stay.
  Ulysses.   You have not patience; come.
  Troilus. I pray you, stay; by hell and all
    hell's torments,
I will not speak a word.
  Diomedes.   And so, good night.
  Cressida. Nay, but you part in anger.
  Troilus.   Doth that grieve thee?
O withered truth!
  Ulysses.   Why, how now, lord!
  Troilus.   By Jove,
I will be patient.
  Cressida.   Guardian! Why, Greek!
  Diomedes. Foh, foh! adieu; you palter.
  Cressida. In faith, I do not; come hither once again. 50
  Ulysses. You shake, my lord, at something; will
    you go?
You will break out.
  Troilus.   She strokes his cheek!
  Ulysses.   Come, come.
  Troilus. Nay, stay; by Jove, I will not speak
    a word;
There is between my will and all offences
A guard of patience. Stay a little while.
  Thersites. How the devil luxury, with his fat rump
and potato-finger, tickles these together! Fry, lechery,
fry!
  Diomedes. But will you then?

60   *Cressida.* In faith, I will, la; never trust me else.
      Diomedes. Give me some token for the surety of it.
      Cressida. I'll fetch you one.   [*goes*
      Ulysses. You have sworn patience.
      Troilus.   Fear me not, sweet lord;
I will not be myself, nor have cognition
Of what I feel. I am all patience.

                   Re-enter CRESSIDA

      Thersites. Now the pledge; now, now, now!
      Cressida. Here, Diomed, keep this sleeve.
                              [*gives him the sleeve*
      Troilus. O beauty! where is thy faith?
      Ulysses.   My lord—
      Troilus. I will be patient; outwardly I will.
70   *Cressida.* You look upon that sleeve; behold it well.
He loved me—O false wench!—Give't me again.
                              [*takes it back*
      Diomedes. Whose was't?
      Cressida. It is no matter, now I have't again.
I will not meet with you tomorrow night.
I prithee, Diomed, visit me no more.
      Thersites. Now she sharpens; well said, whetstone!
      Diomedes. I shall have it.
      Cressida.   What, this?
      Diomedes.   Ay, that.
      Cressida. O, all you gods! O pretty, pretty pledge!
Thy master now lies thinking in his bed
80   Of thee and me, and sighs, and takes my glove,
And gives memorial dainty kisses to it,
As I kiss thee. Nay, do not snatch it from me;
He that takes that doth take my heart withal.
                              [*Diomedes snatches it*
      Diomedes. I had your heart before; this follows it.

Troilus. I did swear patience.

Cressida. You shall not have it, Diomed; faith, you
    shall not;
I'll give you something else.

Diomedes. I will have this. Whose was it?

Cressida.   It is no matter.

Diomedes. Come, tell me whose it was.

Cressida. 'Twas one's that loved me better than
    you will.   90
But now you have it, take it.

Diomedes.   Whose was it?

Cressida. By all Diana's waiting-women yond,
And by herself, I will not tell you whose.

Diomedes. Tomorrow will I wear it on my helm,
And grieve his spirit that dares not challenge it.

Troilus. Wert thou the devil, and wor'st it on
    thy horn,
It should be challenged.

Cressida. Well, well, 'tis done, 'tis past—and yet it
    is not;
I will not keep my word.

Diomedes.   Why then, farewell;
Thou never shalt mock Diomed again.   100

Cressida. You shall not go; one cannot speak a word,
But it straight starts you.

Diomedes.   I do not like this fooling.

Troilus. Nor I, by Pluto; but that that likes not you
Pleases me best.

Diomedes.   What, shall I come? the hour?

Cressida. Ay, come. O Jove! do come; I shall
    be plagued.

Diomedes. Farewell till then.

Cressida.   Good night; I prithee, come.
                                        [*Diomedes goes*

Troilus, farewell! One eye yet looks on thee,
But with my heart the other eye doth see.
Ah, poor our sex! this fault in us I find,
110 The error of our eye directs our mind;
What error leads must err—O, then conclude
Minds swayed by eyes are full of turpitude.   [goes
    Thersites. A proof of strength she could not
        publish more,
    Unless she said 'My mind is now turned whore'.
    Ulysses. All's done, my lord.
    Troilus.   It is.
    Ulysses.   Why stay we then?
    Troilus. To make a recordation to my soul
Of every syllable that here was spoke.
But if I tell how these two did co-act,
Shall I not lie in publishing a truth?
120 Sith yet there is a credence in my heart,
An esperance so obstinately strong,
That doth invert th'attest of eyes and ears;
As if those organs had deceptious functions,
Created only to calumniate.
Was Cressid here?
    Ulysses.   I cannot conjure, Trojan.
    Troilus. She was not, sure.
    Ulysses.   Most sure she was.
    Troilus. Why, my negation hath no taste
        of madness.
    Ulysses. Nor mine, my lord; Cressid was here
        but now.
    Troilus. Let it not be believed for womanhood!
130 Think we had mothers. Do not give advantage
To stubborn critics, apt without a theme
For depravation, to square the general sex
By Cressid's rule; rather think this not Cressid.

Ulysses. What hath she done, prince, that can soil
    our mothers?
Troilus. Nothing at all, unless that this were she.
Thersites. Will 'a swagger himself out on's own eyes?
Troilus. This she? No; this is Diomed's Cressida.
If beauty have a soul, this is not she;
If souls guide vows, if vows be sanctimonies,
If sanctimony be the gods' delight,   140
If there be rule in unity itself,
This is not she. O madness of discourse,
That cause sets up with and against itself!
Bifold authority! where reason can revolt
Without perdition, and loss assume all reason
Without revolt. This is, and is not, Cressid!
Within my soul there doth conduce a fight
Of this strange nature, that a thing inseparate
Divides more wider than the sky and earth;
And yet the spacious breadth of this division   150
Admits no orifex for a point as subtle
As Ariachne's broken woof to enter.
Instance, O instance! strong as Pluto's gates:
Cressid is mine, tied with the bonds of heaven.
Instance, O instance! strong as heaven itself:
The bonds of heaven are slipped, dissolved
    and loosed,
And with another knot, five-finger-tied,
The fractions of her faith, orts of her love,
The fragments, scraps, the bits and greasy relics
Of her o'ereaten faith are given to Diomed.   160
Ulysses. May worthy Troilus be but half attached
With that which here his passion doth express?
Troilus. Ay, Greek; and that shall be divulgéd well
In characters as red as Mars his heart
Inflamed with Venus. Never did young man fancy

With so eternal and so fixed a soul.
Hark, Greek: as much as I do Cressid love,
So much by weight hate I her Diomed.
That sleeve is mine that he'll bear on his helm.
170 Were it a casque composed by Vulcan's skill,
My sword should bite it. Not the dreadful spout
Which shipmen do the hurricano call,
Constringed in mass by the almighty sun,
Shall dizzy with more clamour Neptune's ear
In his descent, than shall my prompted sword
Falling on Diomed.
    Thersites. He'll tickle it for his concupy.
    Troilus. O Cressid! O false Cressid! false,
      false, false!
Let all untruths stand by thy stainéd name,
180 And they'll seem glorious.
    Ulysses.   O, contain yourself;
Your passion draws ears hither.

Enter ÆNEAS

    Æneas. I have been seeking you this hour, my lord.
Hector by this is arming him in Troy;
Ajax your guard stays to conduct you home.
    Troilus. Have with you, prince. My cou.teous
      lord, adieu.
Farewell, revolted fair! and, Diomed,
Stand fast, and wear a castle on thy head!
    Ulysses. I'll bring you to the gates.
    Troilus. Accept distracted thanks.
                  [*Troilus, Æneas, and Ulysses go*
190   *Thersites.* Would I could meet that rogue Diomed! I
would croak like a raven; I would bode, I would bode.
Patroclus will give me anything for the intelligence of
this whore; the parrot will not do more for an almond

than he for a commodious drab. Lechery, lechery!
Still wars and lechery! Nothing else holds fashion.
A burning devil take them!   [*goes*

[5. 3.]   *Troy. Before Priam's palace*

Enter HECTOR and ANDROMACHE

Andromache. When was my lord so much
    ungently tempered,
To stop his ears against admonishment?
Unarm, unarm, and do not fight today.
  Hector. You train me to offend you; get you in.
By all the everlasting gods, I'll go!
  Andromache. My dreams will sure prove ominous to
    the day.
  Hector. No more, I say.

Enter CASSANDRA

  Cassandra.   Where is my brother Hector?
  Andromache. Here, sister; armed, and bloody
    in intent.
Consort with me in loud and dear petition;
Pursue we him on knees; for I have dreamed   10
Of bloody turbulence, and this whole night
Hath nothing been but shapes and forms of slaughter.
  Cassandra. O, 'tis true.
  Hector.   Ho! bid my trumpet sound!
  Cassandra. No notes of sally, for the heavens,
    sweet brother.
  Hector. Be gone, I say. The gods have heard
    me swear.
  Cassandra. The gods are deaf to hot and peevish vows:

They are polluted offerings, more abhorred
Than spotted livers in the sacrifice.

Andromache. O, be persuaded! Do not count it holy
20 To hurt by being just; it is as lawful,
For we would give much, to use violent thefts
And rob in the behalf of charity.

Cassandra. It is the purpose that makes strong the vow;
But vows to every purpose must not hold.
Unarm, sweet Hector.

Hector.   Hold you still, I say;
Mine honour keeps the weather of my fate.
Life every man holds dear; but the dear man
Holds honour far more precious-dear than life.

Enter TROILUS

How now, young man! Mean'st thou to fight today?
30 *Andromache.* Cassandra, call my father to persuade.
                              [*Cassandra goes*
Hector. No, faith, young Troilus; doff thy
        harness, youth;
I am today i'th'vein of chivalry.
Let grow thy sinews till their knots be strong,
And tempt not yet the brushes of the war.
Unarm thee, go; and doubt thou not, brave boy,
I'll stand today for thee and me and Troy.

Troilus. Brother, you have a vice of mercy in you,
Which better fits a lion than a man.

Hector. What vice is that? Good Troilus, chide me
        for it.
40 *Troilus.* When many times the captive Grecian falls,
Even in the fan and wind of your fair sword,
You bid them rise and live.

Hector. O, 'tis fair play.

Troilus.   Fool's play, by heaven, Hector.

Hector. How now! how now!

Troilus.   For th'love of all the gods,
Let's leave the hermit pity with our mother;
And when we have our armours buckled on,
The venomed vengeance ride upon our swords,
Spur them to ruthful work, rein them from ruth!

Hector. Fie, savage, fie!

Troilus.   Hector, then 'tis wars.

Hector. Troilus, I would not have you fight today.   50

Troilus. Who should withhold me?
Not fate, obedience, nor the hand of Mars
Beckoning with fiery truncheon my retire;
Not Priamus and Hecuba on knees,
Their eyes o'ergallèd with recourse of tears;
Nor you, my brother, with your true sword drawn,
Opposed to hinder me, should stop my way,
But by my ruin.

Re-enter CASSANDRA, *with* PRIAM

Cassandra. Lay hold upon him, Priam, hold him fast;
He is thy crutch; now if thou lose thy stay,   60
Thou on him leaning, and all Troy on thee,
Fall all together.

Priam.   Come, Hector, come, go back.
Thy wife hath dreamed; thy mother hath had visions;
Cassandra doth foresee; and I myself
Am like a prophet suddenly enrapt,
To tell thee that this day is ominous;
Therefore, come back.

Hector.   Æneas is afield;
And I do stand engaged to many Greeks,
Even in the faith of valour, to appear
This morning to them.

Priam.   Ay, but thou shalt not go.   70

8   PST&C

Hector. I must not break my faith.
You know me dutiful; therefore, dear sir,
Let me not shame respect, but give me leave
To take that course by your consent and voice
Which you do here forbid me, royal Priam.
 Cassandra. O Priam, yield not to him!
 Andromache.   Do not, dear father.
 Hector. Andromache, I am offended with you;
Upon the love you bear me, get you in.   [*she goes*
 Troilus. This foolish, dreaming, superstitious girl
80 Makes all these bodements.
 Cassandra.   O, farewell, dear Hector!
Look how thou diest! look how thy eye turns pale!
Look how thy wounds do bleed at many vents!
Hark how Troy roars! how Hecuba cries out!
How poor Andromache shrills her dolours forth!
Behold, distraction, frenzy, and amazement,
Like witless antics, one another meet,
And all cry 'Hector! Hector's dead! O Hector!'
 Troilus. Away! away!
 Cassandra. Farewell—yet soft! Hector, I take
  my leave;
90 Thou dost thyself and all our Troy deceive.   [*goes*
 Hector. You are amazed, my liege, at her exclaims.
Go in and cheer the town; we'll forth and fight,
Do deeds worth praise and tell you them at night.
 Priam. Farewell. The gods with safety stand
  about thee!
       [*Priam and Hector go severally; alarum*
 Troilus. They are at it, hark! Proud Diomed, believe,
I come to lose my arm, or win my sleeve.

        Enter PANDARUS

 Pandarus. Do you hear, my lord? do you hear?

Troilus. What now?

Pandarus. Here's a letter come from yon poor girl.

Troilus. Let me read.   -   100

Pandarus. A whoreson tisick, a whoreson rascally
tisick so troubles me, and the foolish fortune of this
girl; and what one thing, what another, that I shall
leave you one o'these days. And I have a rheum in
mine eyes too, and such an ache in my bones that,
unless a man were cursed, I cannot tell what to think
on't. What says she there?

  Troilus. Words, words, mere words; no matter
      from the heart;

Th'effect doth operate another way. [*tearing the letter*

Go, wind, to wind! there turn and change together.   110

My love with words and errors still she feeds,

But edifies another with her deeds.   [*they go severally*

[5. 4.]   *The field between Troy and the Greek camp*

Alarums. Excursions. Enter THERSITES

Thersites. Now they are clapper-clawing one another;
I'll go look on. That dissembling abominable varlet,
Diomed, has got that same scurvy doting foolish young
knave's sleeve of Troy there in his helm. I would fain
see them meet; that that same young Trojan ass, that
loves the whore there, might send that Greekish whore-
masterly villain with the sleeve back to the dissembling
luxurious drab of a sleeveless errand. O't'other side,
the policy of those crafty-swearing rascals, that stale old
mouse-eaten dry cheese, Nestor, and that same dog-fox, 10
Ulysses, is proved not worth a blackberry. They set me
up in policy that mongrel cur, Ajax, against that dog of

as bad a kind, Achilles; and now is the cur Ajax prouder
than the cur Achilles, and will not arm today; whereupon the Grecians begin to proclaim barbarism, and
policy grows into an ill opinion. Soft! here comes sleeve,
and t'other.

Enter DIOMEDES, TROILUS following

Troilus. Fly not; for shouldst thou take the river Styx,
I would swim after.
    Diomedes.   Thou dost miscall retire;
20 I do not fly; but advantageous care
Withdrew me from the odds of multitude.
Have at thee!
    Thersites. Hold thy whore, Grecian! Now for thy
whore, Trojan! Now the sleeve, now the sleeve!
                    [*Troilus and Diomedes go off fighting*

Enter HECTOR

Hector. What art thou, Greek? Art thou for
        Hector's match?
Art thou of blood and honour?
    Thersites. No, no; I am a rascal; a scurvy railing
knave; a very filthy rogue.
    Hector. I do believe thee. Live.   [*goes*
30 *Thersites.* God-a-mercy, that thou wilt believe me;
but a plague break thy neck for frighting me! What's
become of the wenching rogues? I think they have
swallowed one another. I would laugh at that miracle;
yet in a sort lechery eats itself. I'll seek them.   [*goes*

[5. 5.]   *Another part of the field*

Enter DIOMEDES *and Servant*

Diomedes. Go, go, my servant, take thou
        Troilus' horse;
Present the fair steed to my lady Cressid.
Fellow, commend my service to her beauty;
Tell her I have chastised the amorous Trojan,
And am her knight by proof.
        Servant.   I go, my lord.   [*goes*

Enter AGAMEMNON

Agamemnon. Renew, renew! The fierce Polydamas
Hath beat down Menon; bastard Margarelon
Hath Doreus prisoner,
And stands colossus-wise, waving his beam,
Upon the pashéd corpses of the kings   10
Epistrophus and Cedius; Polyxenes is slain;
Amphimachus and Thoas deadly hurt;
Patroclus ta'en or slain; and Palamedes
Sore hurt and bruised; the dreadful sagittary
Appals our numbers; haste we, Diomed,
To reinforcement, or we perish all.   [*goes*

· *Enter* NESTOR *and other Greeks*

Nestor. Go, bear Patroclus' body to Achilles,
And bid the snail-paced Ajax arm for shame. [*some go*
There is a thousand Hectors in the field:
Now here he fights on Galathe his horse,   20
And there lacks work; anon he's there afoot,
And there they fly or die, like scaléd sculls
Before the belching whale; then is he yonder,
And there the strawy Greeks, ripe for his edge,

Fall down before him, like a mower's swath;
Here, there and everywhere he leaves and takes,
Dexterity so obeying appetite
That what he will he does, and does so much
That proof is called impossibility.

Enter ULYSSES

30   *Ulysses.* O, courage, courage, princes!
          great Achilles
Is arming, weeping, cursing, vowing vengeance;
Patroclus' wounds have roused his drowsy blood,
Together with his mangled Myrmidons,
That noseless, handless, hacked and chipped, come
          to him,
Crying on Hector. Ajax hath lost a friend,
And foams at mouth, and he is armed and at it,
Roaring for Troilus; who hath done today
Mad and fantastic execution,
Engaging and redeeming of himself
40 With such a careless force and forceless care
As if that luck, in very spite of cunning,
Bade him win all.

Enter AJAX

Ajax. Troilus! thou coward Troilus!   [*goes*
Diomedes.   Ay, there, there. [*follows*
Nestor. So, so, we draw together.

Enter ACHILLES

Achilles.   Where is this Hector?
Come, come, thou boy-queller, show me thy face;
Know what it is to meet Achilles angry;
Hector! where's Hector? I will none but Hector.
                                        [*they go*

[5.6.]   *Another part of the field*

Enter AJAX

Ajax. Troilus, thou coward Troilus, show
  thy head!

Enter DIOMEDES

Diomedes. Troilus, I say! where's Troilus?
Ajax.   What wouldst thou?
Diomedes. I would correct him.
Ajax. Were I the general, thou shouldst have
  my office
Ere that correction. Troilus, I say! what, Troilus!

Enter TROILUS

Troilus. O traitor Diomed! Turn thy false face,
  thou traitor,
And pay the life thou ow'st me for my horse.
Diomedes. Ha! art thou there?
Ajax. I'll fight with him alone; stand, Diomed.
Diomedes. He is my prize; I will not look upon.   10
Troilus. Come both you cogging Greeks; have at
  you both!   [*they go, fighting*

Enter HECTOR

Hector. Yea, Troilus? O, well fought, my
  youngest brother!

Enter ACHILLES

Achilles. Now do I see thee; ha! have at
  thee, Hector!   [*they fight*
Hector. Pause, if thou wilt.
Achilles. I do disdain thy courtesy, proud Trojan.
Be happy that my arms are out of use;

My rest and negligence befriends thee now,
But thou anon shalt hear of me again;
Till when, go seek thy fortune.   [*goes*

    Hector.   Fare thee well.
20 I would have been much more a fresher man,
Had I expected thee.

Re-enter TROILUS

        How now, my brother!
  Troilus. Ajax hath ta'en Æneas. Shall it be?
No, by the flame of yonder glorious heaven,
He shall not carry him; I'll be ta'en too,
Or bring him off. Fate, hear me what I say!
I reck not though thou end my life today.   [*goes*

Enter one in sumptuous armour

  Hector. Stand, stand, thou Greek; thou art a
    goodly mark.
No? wilt thou not? I like thy armour well;
I'll frush it and unlock the rivets all,
30 But I'll be master of it. [*the Greek flees*] Wilt thou
    not, beast, abide?
Why then, fly on; I'll hunt thee for thy hide.
                  [*goes after*

[5. 7.]   *Another part of the field*

Enter ACHILLES, *with Myrmidons*

  Achilles. Come here about me, you my Myrmidons;
Mark what I say. Attend me where I wheel;
Strike not a stroke, but keep yourselves in breath,
And when I have the bloody Hector found
Empale him with your weapons round about;

In fellest manner execute your arms.
Follow me, sirs, and my proceedings eye;
It is decreed Hector the great must die.   [*they go*

Enter MENELAUS and PARIS, *fighting;* then THERSITES

Thersites. The cuckold and the cuckold-maker are at
it. Now, bull! now, dog! 'Loo, Paris, 'loo! now, my   10
double-horned Spartan! 'loo, Paris, 'loo! The bull has
the game. Ware horns, ho!   [*Paris and Menelaus go*

Enter MARGARELON

Margarelon. Turn, slave, and fight.
Thersites. What art thou?
Margarelon. A bastard son of Priam's.
Thersites. I am a bastard too; I love bastards. I am
a bastard begot, bastard instructed, bastard in mind,
bastard in valour, in everything illegitimate. One bear
will not bite another, and wherefore should one
bastard? Take heed; the quarrel's most ominous to us;   20
if the son of a whore fight for a whore, he tempts
judgement. Farewell, bastard.   [*goes*
Margarelon. The devil take thee, coward!   [*goes*

[5. 8.]   *Another part of the field*

Enter HECTOR

Hector. Most putrefiéd core, so fair without,
Thy goodly armour thus hath cost thy life.
Now is my day's work done. I'll take good breath.
Rest, sword; thou hast thy fill of blood and death.
                                        [*disarms*

Enter ACHILLES *and Myrmidons*

Achilles. Look, Hector, how the sun begins to set,
How ugly night comes breathing at his heels;
Even with the vail and darking of the sun,
To close the day up, Hector's life is done.
Hector. I am unarmed; forego this vantage, Greek.
10 *Achilles.* Strike, fellows, strike; this is the man
   I seek.   *[Hector falls*
So, Ilion, fall thou next! now, Troy, sink down!
Here lies thy heart, thy sinews, and thy bone.
On, Myrmidons, and cry you all amain
'Achilles hath the mighty Hector slain'.
          [retreat sounded
Hark! a retire upon our Grecian part.
Myrmidon. The Trojan trumpets sound the like,
  my lord.
Achilles. The dragon wing of night o'erspreads
  the earth,
And stickler-like the armies separates.
My half-supped sword that frankly would have fed,
20 Pleased with this dainty bait, thus goes to bed.
        [sheathes his sword
Come, tie his body to my horse's tail;
Along the field I will the Trojan trail.
       [they go; retreat sounded

[5. 9.]   *Another part of the field*

 Enter AGAMEMNON, AJAX, MENELAUS, NESTOR,
 DIOMEDES, *and the rest, marching. Shouts within.*

Agamemnon. Hark! hark! what shout is that?
Nestor. Peace, drums!

Soldiers [*within*]. Achilles! Achilles! Hector's
    slain! Achilles!
Diomedes. The bruit is Hector's slain, and
    by Achilles.
Ajax. If it be so, yet bragless let it be;
Great Hector was as good a man as he.
Agamemnon. March patiently along. Let one be sent
To pray Achilles see us at our tent.
If in his death the gods have us befriended,
Great Troy is ours, and our sharp wars are ended.   10
                                   [*they march off*

[5. 10.]   *Another part of the field*

    Enter ÆNEAS, PARIS, ANTENOR, and DEIPHOBUS

Æneas. Stand, ho! yet are we masters of the field.
Never go home; here starve we out the night.

                Enter TROILUS

Troilus. Hector is slain.
All.   Hector! The gods forbid!
Troilus. He's dead; and at the murderer's horse's tail
In beastly sort dragged through the shameful field.
Frown on, you heavens, effect your rage with speed!
Sit, gods, upon your thrones and smite at Troy!
I say, at once let your brief plagues be mercy,
And linger not our sure destructions on! -
Æneas. My lord, you do discomfort all the host.   10
Troilus. You understand me not that tell me so;
I do not speak of flight, of fear, of death,
But dare all imminence that gods and men
Address their dangers in. Hector is gone:
Who shall tell Priam so, or Hecuba?

Let him that will a screech-owl aye be called:
Go in to Troy and say there 'Hector's dead',
There is a word will Priam turn to stone,
Make wells and Niobes of the maids and wives,
20 Cold statues of the youth, and, in a word,
Scare Troy out of itself. But march away.
Hector is dead; there is no more to say.
Stay yet. You vile abominable tents,
Thus proudly pight upon our Phrygian plains,
Let Titan rise as early as he dare,
I'll through and through you! and thou
        great-sized coward,
No space of earth shall sunder our two hates;
I'll haunt thee like a wicked conscience still,
That mouldeth goblins swift as frenzy's thoughts.
30 Strike a free march to Troy! with comfort go:
Hope of revenge shall hide our inward woe.
                                    [*Æneas and Trojans go*

Enter PANDARUS

  Pandarus. But hear you, hear you!
  Troilus. Hence, broker-lackey! ignomy and shame
Pursue thy life, and live aye with thy name!   [*goes*
  Pandarus. A goodly medicine for my aching bones!
O world! world! world! thus is the poor agent despised!
O traders and bawds, how earnestly are you set a-work,
and how ill requited! Why should our endeavour be so
desired and the performance so loathed? What verse
40 for it? what instance for it? Let me see:

      Full merrily the humble-bee doth sing
      Till he hath lost his honey and his sting;
      And being once subdued in arméd tail,
      Sweet honey and sweet notes together fail.

Good traders in the flesh, set this in your painted cloths:
As many as be here of Pandar's hall,
Your eyes, half out, weep out at Pandar's fall;
Or if you cannot weep, yet give some groans,
Though not for me, yet for your aching bones.
Brethren and sisters of the hold-door trade,   50
Some two months hence my will shall here be made.
It should be now, but that my fear is this,
Some galléd goose of Winchester would hiss.
Till then I'll sweat and seek about for eases,
And at that time bequeath you my diseases.   [*goes*

GLOSSARY

Note. Where there is equivocation the meanings are distinguished by (*a*) and (*b*)

'A, he; 1. 2. 77, etc.

A', have; 2. 3. 24, etc.

ABRUPTION, breaking off (in speech), aposiopesis; 3. 2. 65

ACCENT, utterance, voice; 1. 3. 53

ACHIEVEMENT, attainment; 1. 2. 294; 4. 2. 69

ADAMANT, loadstone, magnet; 3. 2. 178

ADDITION, (i) distinctive title, style of address, attribute; 1. 2. 20; 2. 3. 244; 3. 2. 93; (ii) 'something added to a coat of arms, as a mark of honour' (O.E.D. 5); 4. 5. 141 (see note)

ADDRESS, prepare; 4. 4. 146; 5. 10. 14

ADVANCÉD, uplifted, raised; 4. 5. 188

ADVANTAGE, favourable opportunity; 2. 2. 204; 3. 3. 2; 5. 2. 130

ADVERSITY, contrariness, (concr.) quibbler; 5. 1. 12

ADVERTISE, inform; 2. 2. 211

AFFECT, love; 2. 2. 195; 4. 5. 178

AFFECTED, loved; 2. 2. 60 (see note)

AFFECTION, feeling (as opposed to reason), passion; 2. 2. 177

AFFINED, related; 1. 3. 25

AFFRONT, front, meet; 3. 2. 165

AGAINST, in expectation of; 1. 2. 177

AIR, breath, speech; 1. 3. 66

AIRY, (*a*) lofty, (*b*) in everyone's mouth (cf. *aura popularis*); 1. 3. 144

ALARUM, call to arms (usu. by drums); 1. 1. 90 S.D., etc.

ALLOW, commend (O.E.D. 1); 3. 2. 90

ALLOWANCE, commendation, praise; 1. 3. 376; 2. 3. 136

AMAZE, bewilder, stupify; 5. 3. 91

AMAZEMENT, consternation; 2. 2. 210; 5. 3. 85

AN (conj.), if; 1. 1. 43, etc.

ANSWER (sb.), acceptance (of a challenge); 1. 3. 332

ANSWER (vb.), (i) satisfy; 1. 3. 15; (ii) accept (a challenge); 2. 1. 126; 3. 3. 35; 4. 4. 132

ANTIC, grotesque, clown; 5. 3. 86

ANTIQUARY, ancient; 2. 3. 248

APPERTAINMENT, prerogative; 2. 3. 79

APPETITE, (i) self-indulgence; 1. 3. 120, 121; (ii) desire, inclination; 3. 3. 238; 5. 5. 27

APPLY, interpret; 1. 3. 32 (see note)

APPOINTMENT, equipment; 4. 5. 1

APPREHEND, perceive; 3. 2. 73; 3. 3. 124

APPREHENSION, grasp, (*a*) physical arrest, (*b*) mental perception; 2. 3. 114 (see note)

APPROVE, attest; 3. 2. 173

APT, ready; 5. 2. 131

AQUILON, the north or north-north-east wind; 4. 5. 9

ARGUMENT, (i) theme; Prol. 25; (ii) theme of contention; 1. 1. 94; 2. 3. 71, 94, 95, 96; (iii) reason; 4. 5. 26, 27; (iv) (*a*) as in (iii), (*b*) as in (ii); 4. 5. 29

ART, acquired skill, 4. 4. 78

ARTIST, one learned in the liberal arts, scholar; 1. 3. 24

As (conj.), as if; 1. 1. 37; 1. 2. 7; 1. 3. 391; 3. 3. 167; 4. 5. 238

ASSINEGO (dim. of Sp. *asno*=ass), young ass, fool; 2. 1. 43

ASSUBJUGATE, subjugate; 2. 3. 190

ASSUME, lay claim to; 5. 2. 145

ATTACH, seize, lay hold of; (fig.) 5. 2. 161

ATTACHMENT, arrest; (fig.) 4. 2. 5

ATTAINT, blemish; 1. 2. 25

ATTEST (sb.), testimony; 5. 2. 122

ATTEST (vb.), call to witness; 2. 2. 132

ATTRIBUTE, reputation; 2. 3. 115

ATTRIBUTIVE, tributary; 2. 2. 58

AUTHENTIC, authoritative; 1. 3. 108; 3. 2. 180

AUTHOR, originator, prototype; 3. 2. 180

AVOID, (*a*) (*law*) invalidate, (*b*) get rid of; 2. 2. 65

AXLE-TREE, axle-beam, axis of revolution; 1. 3. 66 (see note)

BAIT, (*a*) refreshment, snack, (*b*) a lawyer's 'refresher' (i.e. an extra fee paid to counsel in prolonged or frequently adjourned cases); 5. 8. 20

BATTLE, army; 3. 2. 28

BAUBLE, toylike, insignificant; 1. 3. 35

BAY, bark; (fig.) 2. 3. 89

BEAM, spear (with allusion to Goliath's spear, the staff of which was like a weaver's beam, 1. Sam. xvii. 7); 5. 5. 9

BEAR IT, behave, act; 2. 3. 215

BEAVER, face-guard of a helmet; 1. 3. 296

BEEF-WITTED, dull-brained; 2. 1. 13 (see note)

BEGUILE, defraud, rob; 4. 4. 35

BEHALF; 'in my behalf'=for my benefit; 3. 3. 16

BELCH, spout; 5. 5. 23

BELLY, swell; 2. 2. 74

BEND, (i) arch; 1. 3. 379 (see note); (ii) turn; 3. 3. 43; 4. 4. 139

BENDING, courteous, gracious; 1. 3. 236

BENEFIT, favour; 3. 3. 14

BENT, inclination; (of the ears) 1. 3. 252; (of the eyes) 4. 5. 282

BESEECH, entreaty; 1. 2. 294

BESTOWING, employment, use; 3. 2. 37

BIAS (adj.), puffed out on one side (with allusion to the bias of a bowl); 4. 5. 8

BIAS (adv.), awry; 1. 3. 15

BIAS-DRAWING (sb.), inclination; 4. 5. 169

BIFOLD, twofold; 5. 2. 144

BLANK, document with spaces left blank to be filled up at the pleasure of the recipient, carte blanche; 3. 3. 231

BLESS, guard, keep; 2. 3. 28

BLOOD, (i) the supposed seat of emotions, passions, 'humours', etc.; Prol. 2; 2. 2. 169; 2. 3. 29, 210; 5. 1. 47, 49; (ii) noble descent; 3. 3. 26; 5. 4. 26; (iii) kinship, stock; 4. 2. 98; 4. 5. 83

BLOW UP, swell; 1. 3. 317 (see note)

BOB, (i) (a) bamboozle, (b) (perh. of diff. etymol.) buffet; 2. 1. 68; (ii) cheat; 3. 1. 69

BODEMENT, foreboding; 5. 3. 80

BOLTING, sifting; 1. 1. 19, 21

BOOK, 'without book'= by heart; 2. 1. 18

BOOT, something given in addition; (i) 'to boot'= into the bargain; 1. 2. 240; (ii) premium, odds; 4. 5. 40

BOREAS, the north wind; 1. 3. 38

BORROW, be indebted for, derive; 4. 5. 133

BOTCH, ulcer; 5. 1. 5

BOTCHY, ulcerous; 2. 1. 6

BOURN, boundary; 2. 3. 246

BOWELS, considered as the seat of the tender emotions, (hence) compassion, mercy; 2. 1. 48; 2. 2. 11

BOY-QUELLER, boy-killer; 5. 5. 45

BRATCH, bitch hound; (fig.) 2. 1. 113

BRAVE (adj.), splendid; Prol. 15; 1. 2. 186

BRAVE (sb.), bravado, defiance; 4. 4. 137

BRAVELY, excellently, famously; 1. 2. 183; 3. 3. 213

BRAWN, muscle (esp. the fleshy muscles of the arm and leg); 1. 3. 297

BREATH, (i) speech (with quibble on the lit. sense); 2. 2. 74; (ii) breathing-space, pause; 2. 3. 111; 4. 5. 92

BREESE, gadfly; 1. 3. 48

BRIAREUS, in Gk. myth. a monster with a hundred arms; 1. 2. 28

BRING, (i) 'to bring'; 1. 2. 280 (see WITH); (ii) 'bring off'= preserve, rescue; 1. 3. 334; 5. 6. 25; (iii) 'bring forth'= utter; 1. 3. 242

BROKEN, (a) (of music) employing different families of instruments, (b) interrupted; 3. 1. 50 (see note)

BROKER-BETWEEN, BROKER-LACKEY, pandar; 3. 2. 202–3; 5. 10. 33

BROTHERHOOD, fraternity, guild; 1. 3. 104

BRUIT, noise, report; 5. 9. 4

BRUSH, encounter, clash; 5. 3. 34

BUCKLE IN, confine; 2. 2. 30

BURDEN, freight of a ship; 1. 3. 71

BUSS, kiss; 4. 5. 220

BUTT, cask; 5. 1. 27

BUY, (fig.) be an equivalent for; 3. 3. 28

CANCER, the Crab, the fourth sign of the zodiac, entered by the sun on 21 June; 2. 3. 194

CAPOCCHIA (*It.*), simpleton; 4. 3. 32

CAPTIVE, vanquished; 5. 3. 40

CARRY, (i) bear away as a prize; 5. 6. 24; (ii) 'carry it'=have the mastery; 2. 3. 2, 216

CASQUE, helmet; 5. 2. 170

CATLING, catgut, the smallest sized strings of musical instruments; 3. 3. 303

CENTRE, the earth (as the supposed centre of the universe); 1. 3. 85

CHAFE, heat, become angry; Prol. 2; 1. 2. 167; 4. 5. 260

CHALLENGE, lay claim to, contest; 5. 2. 95, 97

CHANCE (sb.), (i) fortune (good or bad); Prol. 31; (ii) misfortune; 1. 3. 33; (iii) good fortune, luck; 3. 3. 131

CHANCE (vb.), happen; 'how chance'=how chances it that; 3. 1. 138

CHANGE (sb. & vb.), exchange; 3. 3. 27; 4. 2. 91

CHAPMAN, trader; 4. 1. 77

CHARACTER, (i) graphic symbol, figure; 1. 3. 325; (ii) distinctive mark, brand; 5. 2. 164

CHARACTERLESS, leaving no mark; 3. 2. 187

CHARGE, cost; 4. 1. 59

CHERUBIN, cherub; 3. 2. 68

CHIDE, quarrel, brawl; 1. 3. 54

CHIVALRY, (i) knighthood; 1. 2. 230; (ii) prowess in war, bravery; 4. 4. 148; 5. 3. 32

CHOLLER, jowl; 4. 5. 9 (see note)

CIRCUMSTANCE, particulars (of a discourse); 3. 3. 114

CIRCUMVENTION, strategy; 2. 3. 15

CLAPPER-CLAW, maul; 5. 4. 1

CLEF, (*a*) key in music, (*b*) (etymol. a diff. word) cleft, fork of the legs; 5. 2. 12

CLOSE, (*a*) come to terms, (*b*) come close; 3. 2. 48

CLOSET, private apartment, study; 'closet-war' (nonce use)=study warfare; 1. 3. 205

CLOTH, 'painted cloth'= 'hanging for a room painted or worked with figures, mottoes or texts; tapestry' (O.E.D.); 5. 10. 45

CLOTPOLL, blockhead; 2. 1. 116

CO-ACT, act together; 5. 2. 118

COBLOAF, little loaf with a round head; 2. 1. 37

COGGING, cheating, deceitful; 5. 6. 11

COGNITION, (*a*) consciousness, (*b*) (*law*) 'the action of taking judicial or authoritative notice' (cf. O.E.D. 3); 5. 2. 64

COLDLY, chastely; 1. 3. 229

COLOSSUS-WISE, like the Colossus (a gigantic statue of Apollo, alleged to have spanned the harbour of Rhodes); 5. 5. 9

COME TO IT, reach maturity; 1. 2. 84, 85

COMFORT, encouragement (O.E.D. 1); 5. 10. 30

COMMERCE, transactions; 3. 3. 205

COMMIXTION, commixture; 4. 5. 124

9

COMMODIOUS, accommodating; 5. 2. 194 (see note)

COMMOTION, (a) public disorder, (b) mental perturbation; 2. 3. 173

COMPARE, comparison; 3. 2. 174

COMPASSED, 'compassed window'=semicircular bay window; 1. 2. 112

COMPLETE, perfectly endowed, accomplished; 3. 3. 181

COMPLIMENTAL, complimentary; 3. 1. 40

COMPOSED, made; 5. 2. 170

COMPOSURE, (i) combination; 2. 3. 98; (ii) temperament, disposition; 2. 3. 237

CON, learn by heart; 2. 1. 17

CONCEIT, understanding; 1. 3. 153

CONCUPY, concupiscence; 5. 2. 177 (see note)

CONDITION, (i) character; Prol. 25; (ii) ellipt.=on condition that, even if; 1. 2. 74; (iii) position, rank; 3. 3. 9

CONDUCE, (intr. for refl.) carry on, go on; 5. 2. 147 (see note)

CONDUCT, guidance; 2. 2. 62

CONFLUX, confluence; 1. 3. 7

CONFOUND, destroy (O.E.D. 1); 2. 3. 74; 3. 1. 118

CONJURE, call up (spirits); 2. 3. 6; 5. 2. 125

CONSIGNED, sealed, added as ratification; 4. 4. 45

CONSISTING, inherent; 3. 3. 116

CONSORT, keep company, join; 5. 3. 9

CONSTRINGE, compress; 5. 2. 173

CONTENTION, combat; 4. 1. 18; 4. 5. 205

CONTRIVE, devise, plan; 1. 3. 201

CONVENIENCE, favourable circumstance, advantage; 3. 3. 7

CONVINCE, convict; 2. 2. 130

CONVIVE, feast together; 4. 5. 272

COPE, (i) come to blows with; 1. 2. 33; (ii) prove a match for; 2. 3. 261

COPPER NOSE, 'a red nose caused by the disease *Acne rosacea*, by intemperance, etc. '(O.E.D.); 1. 2. 107 (see note)

CORE, (i) core of an ulcer; 2. 1. 6; 5. 1. 4; (ii) core of fruit; 5. 8. 1

CO-RIVAL, vie with; 1. 3. 44

CORRECT, chastise; 5. 6. 3

CORRECTION, punishment; 5. 6. 5

CORRESPONSIVE, corresponding; Prol. 18

COUCH, hide; 1. 1. 41

COUNSEL, 'soul of counsel'= inmost thoughts; 3. 2. 132

COUNTER, token (of metal, etc.) used instead of real coins in calculation; 2. 2. 28

COUNTERFEIT, (a) sham, (b) false coin; 2. 3. 24

COUPLE, link, conjoin; 1. 3. 276 (see note)

COURSE, (i) appointed (planetary) course; 1. 3. 87; (ii) complete courses of the sun'=years; 4. 1. 29

COURTESY, obeisance; 2. 3. 105

COUSIN, niece; 1. 2. 42; 3. 1. 35, 84; 3. 2. 2, 7, 198; 4. 2. 24

COUSIN-GERMAN, first cousin; 4. 5. 121

CRAMMED, fatted (for the table); 2. 2. 49

CREST, comb, mane (symbolic of pride); 1. 3. 379

CRITIC, detractor; 5. 2. 131

CROWNET, by-form of 'coronet'; Prol. 6

CRUSTY, scabby; 5. 1. 5

CRY, public acclamation; 3. 3. 184

CRY ON, exclaim against; 5. 5. 35

CUNNING, dexterity, skill; 5. 5. 41

CURIOUS, minutely scanned, minute; 3. 2. 65 (see note)

DAINTY, (i) 'dainty of'= fastidious about; 1. 3. 145; (ii) delightful; 5. 2. 81

DAPHNE, nymph pursued by Apollo; 1. 1. 100

DARDAN, Trojan; Prol. 13

DARKING, darkening; 5. 8. 7 (see note)

DATE, duration, season; 1. 2. 258 (see note)

DAYS, (i) 'by days'=day by day; 4. 1. 10; (ii) in the day (old genitive of time = time when); 4. 5. 12

DEAR, heartfelt, earnest; 5. 3. 9

DEARLY, richly; 3. 3. 96

DEATH-TOKEN, plague-spot betokening approaching death; 2. 3. 175

DEBONAIR, gentle, meek; 1. 3. 235

DECEPTIOUS, deceptive; 5. 2. 123

DECLINE, (i) (a) inflect, (b) refuse; 2. 3. 52 (see note); (ii) fall, descend; 4. 5. 189

DECLINED, fallen, vanquished; 4. 5. 189

DEEM, thought; 4. 4. 59

DEGREE, (i) rank, esp. high rank; 1. 3. 83; (ii) established order of precedence; 1. 3. 108, 125, 127; (iii) (a) as in (ii) with allusion to (b) astronomy; 1. 3. 86; the rung of a ladder; 1. 3. 101; academic rank; 1. 3. 104; music; 1. 3. 109

DEJECT (ppl. a.), dejected, downcast; 2. 2. 50

DEJECT (vb.), depress, lessen; 2. 2. 121

DENY, (i) refuse; 2. 2. 24; 3. 3. 22; (ii) disclaim knowledge of; 4. 2. 49

DEPEND UPON, (a) rely upon, (b) be servant to; 3. 1. 4, 5, 6

DEPENDENT, impending; 2. 3. 19

DEPRAVATION, detraction; 5. 2. 132

DEPUTATION, deputed office; 1. 3. 152

DERACINATE, uproot; 1. 3. 99

DERIVE, show the derivation of, explain; 2. 3. 60

DESIRE, (i) request; 3. 3. 21, 235; (ii) invite; 4. 5. 150

DESPITEFUL, hateful; 4. 1. 34

DETERMINATION, (judicial) decision; 2. 2. 170

DEVICE, contrivance; 1. 3. 374

DEXTER, (heraldic term) right; 4. 5. 128

DIANA, goddess of the moon and chastity, the moon; 5. 2. 92

DIE, (hyperb. and ellipt.) die of laughing; 1. 3. 176

DIGNITY, worthiness; 2. 2. 54

DILATED, extensive; 2. 3. 247

DIMINUTIVE, midget; 5. 1. 33

DIRECTIVE, subject to direction; 1. 3. 356

DISCIPLINE (sb.), instruction (O.E.D. 1); 2. 3. 29

DISCIPLINE (vb.), instruct, train (O.E.D. 1); 2. 3. 241

DISCOMFORT, dishearten; 5. 10. 10

DISCOURSE, (i) 'discourse of reason'=process of reasoning; 2. 2. 116; (ii) reasoning, thought; 5. 2. 142

DISCOVER, reveal; 1. 3. 138; 5. 2. 6

DISCOVERY, revelation, disclosure; 5. 1. 23

DISCRETION, judgement; 1. 2. 23, 252

DISME, dime, a tenth part, 'tithe'; 2. 2. 19

DISORBED, removed from its sphere; 2. 2. 46

DISPOSE, disposition; 2. 3. 162

DISPOSER, manager, mistress; 3. 1. 87 (see note), 89, 92

DISSOLVE, loosen, untie; 5. 2. 156

DISTAIN, sully, dishonour; 1. 3. 241

DISTASTE, (i) dislike; 2. 2. 66; (ii) make distasteful; 2. 2. 123; 4. 4. 48

DISTEMPERED, disordered; 2. 2. 169

DISTINCT, separate; 4. 4. 45

DISTINCTION, discrimination; 1. 3. 27; 3. 2. 27

DISTRACTION, alienation from one's senses; (i) unconsciousness; 3. 2. 23; (ii) madness, frenzy; 5. 2. 42; 5. 3. 85

DIVIDABLE, 'that divides' (On.); 1. 3. 105 (see note)

DIVULGE, proclaim, make known; 5. 2. 163

DIZZY, make dizzy; 5. 2. 174

DO, (i) (imper.) go on, continue; 2. 1. 25, 41, 52, 53; (ii) copulate; 4. 2. 26 (see note)

DOUBT, suspect, fear; 1. 2. 277

DRAUGHT, cesspool, sewer; 5. 1. 73

DRAW, cause to assemble; 2. 3. 72

DRESSED, prepared; 1. 3. 166

DRIFT, intention, aim; 3. 3. 113

DROWSY, sluggish; 2. 2. 210; 5. 5. 32

DRY, barren, sterile; 1. 3. 329 (see note); 2. 3. 221

DULL, inactive; 2. 2. 209

EDIFY, elevate; 5. 3. 112 (see note)

EFFECT, fact, reality; 5. 3. 109

ELD, old age; 2. 2. 104

EMPALE, hem in; 5. 7. 5

EMULATION, jealous rivalry; 1. 3. 134; 2. 2. 212; 3. 3. 156; 4. 5. 123

EMULOUS, (i) envious; 2. 3. 72, 228; 3. 3. 189; (ii) ambitious; 4. 1. 30

ENCOUNTERER, forward person; 4. 5. 58

ENFREED, released; 4. 1. 40

ENGAGE, (i) bind by a pledge; 2. 2. 124; 5. 3. 68; (ii) (a) as in (i), (b) embroil; 5. 5. 39

ENGINE, machine of war; 1. 3. 208; 2. 3. 133

ENGINER, (a) contriver, strategist, (b) maker of military 'engines'; 2. 3. 8

ENLARD, fatten; 2. 3. 193

ENRAPT, carried away, inspired; 5. 3. 65

FILL, shaft of a cart; 3. 2. 45

FINE, exquisite, pure; 3. 2. 23; 4. 4. 3

FINENESS, (i) purity (of metals); 1. 3. 22; (ii) subtlety; 1. 3. 209

FIRSTLING, first product, first-fruits (cf. Gen. iv. 4); Prol. 27

FIT, (a) spasm, (b) strain of music, a stave; 3. 1. 58 (see note)

FITCHEW, polecat; 5. 1. 59

FITNESS, suitable occasion; 1. 3. 202

FIXURE, fixed position; 1. 3. 101

FLAT, (of drink) stale; 4. 1. 64

FLOOD, sea; 1. 1. 104

FLOURISH, fanfare (of trumpets, etc.) for entry or exit in state; 3. 3. S.D., etc.

FOH, exclamation of disgust; 5. 2. 23

FOIL, overthrow, defeat; 1. 3. 371

FOLD, folding, embrace; 3. 3. 223

FOLLY, wantonness; 5. 2. 19

FOND, foolish; 1. 1. 10

FOOL, (a) idiot, (b) a kind of custard; 5. 1. 9

FOOTING, step, tread; 1. 3. 156

FOR (conj.), because; 5. 3. 21

FOR (prep.), (i) against; 1. 2. 269; (ii) denoting the amount staked; 3. 2. 52; (iii) for the sake of; 5. 2. 129

FORCE, stuff, cram; 1. 2. 23; 2. 3. 220; 5. 1. 56

FORCELESS, effortless; 5. 5. 40

FOREHAND, holding the front position; 1. 3. 143

FORESTALL, obstruct, hinder; 1. 3. 199 (see note)

FORFEIT, forfeiture (of life); 4. 5. 187

FORKED, divided like two horns (alluding to cuckoldry); 1. 2. 165

FORM (sb.), (i) regularity, good order; 1. 3. 87; (ii) manner; 3. 3. 51

FORM (vb.), put into shape, frame; 2. 2. 120; 3. 3. 119

FORTH, out (to battle); 1. 2. 221

FORTHRIGHT, straight path; 3. 3. 158

FRACTION, (i) dissension; 2. 3. 97; (ii) fragment; 5. 2. 158

FRANKLY, without restraint, lavishly; 5. 8. 19

FRAUGHTAGE, freight; Prol. 13

FRAY, frighten; 3. 2. 32

FREE, (i) innocent, harmless; 1. 3. 235; (ii) unbiased; 2. 2. 170; (iii) generous; 4. 5. 100, 139

FRIEND, befriend, assist; 1. 2. 78

FRUSH, smash, batter; 5. 6. 29

FULFILLING, tightly fitting; Prol. 18 (see note)

FULL, (i) satisfaction; 3. 3. 241; (ii) 'in the full'=in full company; 4. 5. 272

FUMBLE UP, wrap up clumsily, huddle together; 4. 4. 46

FURNISH, equip; 3. 3. 33

GAGE, bind by formal promise; 5. 1. 40

GAINSAY, forbid; 4. 5. 132

GALL, (i) bitterness, rancour; 1. 3. 193, 237; 2. 2. 144; 4. 5. 30; (ii) applied abusively to a person; 5. 1. 34

GALLANTRY, gallants (collectively); 3. 1. 137

GALLED, (a) affected with 'galls' (=venereal sores), (b) chafed, offended; 5. 10. 53

GAME, amorous sport; 4. 5. 63

GAWD, toy, gewgaw; 3. 3. 176

GEAR, (i) business; 1. 1. 6; (ii) equipment, necessaries; 3. 2. 210

GENERAL (sb.), (i) that which is common to all; 1. 3. 180; (ii) the whole, the multitude; 1. 3. 342

GENERALLY, everywhere; 2. 1. 3

GENERATION, (i) procreation; 3. 1. 132; (ii) progeny; 3. 1. 134

GENEROUS, high-born, noble; 2. 2. 155

GENIUS, 'the tutelary god or attendant spirit allotted to every person at his birth to govern his fortunes and... finally to conduct him out of the world' (O.E.D. 1); 4. 4. 50

GENTLE (adj.), noble; 4. 1. 34

GENTLE (adv.), courteously; 4. 5. 287

GET, beget; 2. 3. 238; 3. 2. 103

GLIMPSE, flash, (fig.) trace; 1. 2. 24

GLOZE, make glosses, comment; 2. 2. 165

GO TO, exclam. of remonstrance; (i) 1. 1. 44; 1. 2. 128; 2. 1. 93; 3. 1. 67; (ii) of encouragement; 3. 2. 52, 196

GOD-A-MERCY, God reward you (an expression of thanks from an inferior); 5. 4. 30

GOD BU'Y YOU, goodbye (a contraction of 'God be with you'); 3. 3. 292

GOOD NOW (interj.), please; 3. 1. 113 (see note)

GOOSE OF WINCHESTER, one affected by a venereal disease known as 'Winchester goose' (with allusion to the Southwark stews formerly under the direction of the Bishop of Winchester); 5. 10. 53

GORGET, piece of armour for the throat; 1. 3. 174

GRACIOUS, righteous, godly; 2. 2. 125

GREAT, full; 'great morning' =broad day; 4. 3. 1

GREEK, 'merry Greek'= wanton; 1. 2. 110

GREEN, (i) (a) the colour, (b) immature; 1. 2. 153; (ii) (a) youthful, (b) immature, foolish; 2. 3. 251

GROSSNESS, bulk, size in full; 1. 3. 325

HAIR, (i) 'against the hair' =against the grain; 1. 2. 26–7; (ii) 'to a hair'=to a nicety; 3. 1. 145

HANDSOMENESS, good manners; 2. 1. 15 (see note)

HANG THE LIP, be downcast; 3. 1. 140

HARDIMENT, boldness; 4. 5. 28

HARNESS, armour; 5. 3. 31

HARNESSED, armed; 1. 2. 8

HASTE, urge on, hurry; 4. 3. 5

HATCHED, engraved; 1. 3. 65 (see note)

HAVE, (i) 'have with you' (a stock reply)=coming, I am ready; 5. 2. 185; (ii) 'have at you' (a stock warning of intended attack); 5. 4. 22; 5. 6. 11, 13

HAVING, possessions, endowments; 3. 3. 97

HAZARD, 'on hazard'=at stake; Prol. 22

HEAP, great company; 'on heaps'=in a mass; 3. 2. 28

HEAVY, sad; 4. 5. 95

HEDGE; (i) 'hedge out'=exclude, fob off; 3. 1. 61 (see note); (ii) 'hedge aside'=shrink away; 3. 3. 158 (see note)

HEEL, dance (cf. LAVOLT); 4. 4. 86

HEIGH-HO, exclam. of dejection, etc.; 3. 1. 127

HEIGHT, 'to the height'=to the utmost; 5. 1. 3

HELM, helmet; 1. 2. 234; 4. 5. 255; 5. 2. 94, 169; 5. 4. 4

HEM, interjection to attract attention; 1. 2. 229

HIS, (i) its (see Abbott, § 228); 1. 3. 75, 207, 210, 241; 2. 2. 54; 3. 3. 123; 5. 2. 175; (ii) 's (see Abbott, § 217); 2. 1. 52; 4. 5. 177, 255; 5. 2. 164

HOLD-DOOR, pandering (cf. Per. G. 'door-keeper', 'hatch'); 5. 10. 50

HONEST, decent; 5. 1. 50

HONESTY, reputation for chastity; 1. 2. 263 (see note)

HORN, cuckold's horn; 1. 1. 114; 4. 5. 31, 46; 5. 7. 12

HOSTESS, landlady of an inn; 3. 3. 252

HOT, (i) violent; 2. 2. 6; (ii) excited, passionate; 2. 2. 116, 169; 2. 3. 171; 3. 1. 130, 131, 132, 133; 5. 3. 16; (iii) eager, keen; 4. 5. 186

How, at what price; 4. 2. 23

HOW NOW, exclam. of expostulation, surprise, welcome; 1. 1. 71, etc.

HOY-DAY, exclam. of surprise; 5. 1. 64

HULK, large ship of burden; 2. 3. 263

HUMANITY, human nature; 2. 2. 175

HUMOROUS, pertaining to the 'humours' (q.v.); 2. 3. 128

HUMOUR, the relative proportions of the four chief fluids of the body, which (acc. to mediev. and Eliz. physiology) determined temperament; 1. 2. 22; 2. 3. 210

HURRICANO, waterspout; 5. 2. 172

HUSBANDRY, a husbandman's care of business; 1. 2. 7

HYPERION, the god of the sun, the sun; 2. 3. 195

IDLE, trifling; 5. 1. 30

IGNOMY, ignominy; 5. 10. 33

ILION, ILIUM, Priam's palace; 1. 1. 103 (see note), etc.

ILL-DISPOSED, indisposed; 2. 3. 76

IMAGE, mental picture, idea; 2. 2. 60

IMBECILITY, weakness; 1. 3. 114

IMMATERIAL, insubstantial, flimsy; 5. 1. 30

IMMINENCE, that which is imminent, impending peril; 5. 10. 13

IMMURE, enclosing wall; Prol. 8

IMPAIR, inferior; 4. 5. 103 (see note)

IMPERIOUS, imperial; 4. 5. 172

IMPORT, be of importance to; 4. 2. 50

IMPORTLESS, unimportant; 1. 3. 71

IMPOSITION, task imposed; 3. 2. 78

IMPOSTUME, abscess; 5. 1. 21

IMPRESS, (a) conscription, (b) impression made by striking; 2. 1. 97

IMPRESSURE, impression, mark; 4. 5. 131

IMPUDENT, shameless; 3. 3. 217

IMPUTATION, reputation; 1. 3. 339

IN (I'), on; 4. 2. 34; 5. 4. 4

INCH, 'to his inches'=(fig.) intimately; 4. 5. 111

INCLUDE, embody; 1. 3. 119 (see note)

INDEX, forefinger, pointer, (hence) prefatory table of contents, prologue; 1. 3. 343

INDIFFERENT, tolerably; 1. 2. 224

INDISTINGUISHABLE, of indeterminate shape, deformed; 5. 1. 28

INDRENCHED, immersed; 1. 1. 53

INFECT (vb.), affect injuriously, impair; 1. 3. 8

INFECT (ppl.), infected; 1. 3. 187

INFINITE (sb.), infinity; 2. 2. 29

INFLUENCE, 'the supposed flowing from the stars or heavens of an etherial fluid acting upon the character and destiny of men, and affecting sublunary things generally' (O.E.D. 2); 1. 3. 92

INSISTURE, steady continuance; 1. 3. 87 (see note)

INSTANCE, (i) cause; 1. 3. 77; (ii) proof, evidence; 5. 2.

153, 155; (iii) example; 5. 10. 40

INSTANT, now present; 3. 3. 153

INTELLIGENCE, news; 5. 2. 192

INTERCHANGEABLY, reciprocally ('formerly freq. in the wording of legal compacts', O.E.D.); 3. 2. 57

IRIS, goddess who, as messenger of the gods, appeared as a rainbow, the rainbow; 1. 3. 379

IRON, weapon; 2. 3. 16

ITCH, 'fingers itch'=have a burning desire (sc. to strike); 2. 1. 25

JADE, ill-tempered horse; (as a term of abuse) 2. 1. 19

JAR, discord; 1. 3. 117

JERKIN, short coat, usually sleeved, leather jerkins being reversible (see Linthicum, pp. 202–3, 240); 3. 3. 264

JUDGEMENT, person of judgement; 1. 2. 192

JUSTNESS, justice, rightfulness; 2. 2. 119

KEEP, (i) keep in, remain in; 1. 3. 190; 2. 3. 256; 5. 1. 10; (ii) stay, dwell; 4. 5. 278

KEN, recognize; 4. 5. 14

KIN, akin; 1. 3. 25; 3. 3. 175

KIND, manner; 2. 3. 127

KINGDOMED, (a) having a kingdom, (b) as a kingdom in himself; 2. 3. 173

KISS, (of bowls) touch one another (cf. MISTRESS); 3. 2. 49

KNOT, hard mass (of muscle), muscle; 5. 3. 33

KNOW, (a) be acquainted with, (b) have sexual intercourse with; 1. 2. 64

LA, exclamation to emphasize a statement; 3. 1. 75; 5. 2. 60
LARDED, interlarded, enriched; 5. 1. 56
LARGE, 'at large'=full sized; 1. 3. 346
LAVOLT, lavolta, 'a lively dance for two persons, consisting a good deal in high and active bounds' (Nares, cited O.E.D.); 4. 4. 86
LEAVE, neglect, omit; 3. 3. 133; 5. 1. 93
LETHARGY, 'a drowsy and forgetful sickness rising of impostumation of cold phlegm putrified, especially in the hinder part of the brain, whereby memory and reason almost utterly perish' (Cooper); 5. 1. 19
LID, eyelid; 'by God's lid', a petty oath; 1. 2. 211
LIEF, dear; 'had as lief'=would as soon; 1. 2. 105
LIFTER, (a) usu. sense, (b) thief; 1. 2. 118 (see note)
LIGHT (adv.), swiftly (O.E.D. 10); 1. 2. 8
LIKE (vb. impers.), please; 5. 2. 103
LIMEKILN, (fig.) burning; 5. 1. 21
LINE, rule, 'principle' (Schmidt); 1. 3. 88
LINGER ON, prolong; 5. 10. 9
LISTS, space enclosed by palisades for tilting, etc.; 4. 5. S.D., 93 S.D.
LIVE, remain; 'live to come' =are to come; 3. 3. 16

LIVER, the supposed seat of the passions, here of courage; 2. 2. 50
'LOO, a cry to incite a dog to the chase; 5. 7. 10, 11
LOOK UPON, be an onlooker; 5. 6. 10
LOOSE, casual, 3. 3. 41; 4. 4. 46
LOVER, well-wisher, friend; 3. 3. 214
LUBBER, (pred.) loutish; 3. 3. 139
LUNES, mad freaks; 2. 3. 129 (see note)
LUST, pleasure; 'to my lust' =with pleasure; 4. 4. 132 (see note)
LUSTIHOOD, bodily vigour; 2. 2. 50
LUXURIOUS, lecherous; 5. 4. 8
LUXURY, lechery; 5. 2. 56

MACULATION, stain of impurity; 4. 4. 64
MAGNANIMOUS, noble, valiant; 2. 2. 200; 3. 3. 275
MAIDEN (adj.), innocent, bloodless; 4. 5. 87
MAIDEN (sb.), a man who has abstained from sexual intercourse; 3. 2. 209
MAIL, piece of mail-armour; 3. 3. 152
MAIN (adj.), general; 1. 3. 372
MAIN (sb.), full might; 2. 3. 259
MAINLY, strongly, very much; 4. 4. 85
MAKE, have to do with (a person or thing); 1. 1. 14, 85
MANAGE, management; 3. 3. 25
MAPPERY (nonce word, contemptuous), map-making; 1. 3. 205

MARK, target; 5. 6. 27

MARRY (a light asseveration, orig. the name of the Virgin Mary), indeed, to be sure; 2. 1. 120; 3. 1. 64

MASS, solid bulk; 1. 3. 29

MASTIC, gummy; 1. 3. 73 (see note)

MATCH, bargain; 4. 5. 37, 270

MATTER, (a) pus, (b) substance, sense; 2. 1. 8

MAY, 'you may'=go on; 3. 1. 109

MEALY, resembling meal, powdery, fragile; 3. 3. 79

MEAT, solid food; 1. 2. 243

MENDS, remedy; 1. 1. 70

MERCURY, Roman god identified with Hermes, the messenger of the gods, whose sandals were fitted with wings and whose staff of office was wreathed with serpents; 2. 2. 45; 2. 3. 11

MERE, absolute; 1. 3. 111, 287

MILO (or MILON), a famous athlete of Crotona of the 6th cent. B.C., said to have carried a bull on his shoulders; 2. 3. 244

MINCED, (a) subdivided minutely, (b) with allusion to 'minced-pie'; 1. 2. 257 (see note)

MINISTER, agent; Prol. 4

MIRABLE, marvellous; 4. 5. 142

MISPRIZE, scorn; 4. 5. 74

MISSION, sending of help (On.); 3. 3. 189

MISTRESS, (a) usu. sense, (b) small bowl, the jack; 3. 2. 49

MODEST, moderate, befitting; 2. 2. 15

MODESTLY, without exaggeration; 4. 5. 222

MOIETY, portion; 2. 2. 107

MONSTRUOSITY (old form of 'monstrosity'), marvel; 3. 2. 80

MONUMENTAL, like a monument; 3. 3. 153

MOTIVE, moving limb or organ; 4. 5. 57

MOUTH, 'spend his mouth', see SPEND; 5. 1. 88–9

MOVE, (i) exhort; 3. 3. 216; (ii) anger; 4. 4. 129

MUCH (adv.), very; 2. 3. 106

MULTIPOTENT, very powerful; 4. 5. 129

MURRAIN, plague; 'a murrain of' (or 'on'), an imprecation; 2. 1. 19

MUTINY, strife, contention; 1. 3. 96

MYRMIDON; 'the great Myrmidon'=Achilles (see next entry) ; 1. 3. 377

MYRMIDONS, warriors from Thessaly brought to Troy by Achilles; 5. 5. 33, etc.

NATURE, human nature; 2. 2. 173, 185; 3. 3. 175

NEAPOLITAN, 'Neapolitan bone-ache'=syphilis (supposedly originating in Naples); 2. 3. 18

NEED (vb.); 'what need'=what need is there for; 5. 1. 12 (see note)

NEGLECTION, neglect; 1. 3. 127

NEGOTIATION, business affair; 3. 3. 24

NEPTUNE, god of the sea, the sea; 1. 3. 45; 5. 2. 174

NERVE, sinew, tendon; (fig.) 1. 3. 55

NICE, precise; 4. 5. 250

NIGHTLY, at night; 4. 4. 73

NIOBE, in Gk. myth. woman turned into a stone column while weeping for her children; her tears continued to flow from the column; 5. 10. 19

NOD, (a) sign of recognition, (b) (etymol. a diff. word) noddy, fool; 1. 2. 196 (see note)

NOISE, report, rumour; 1. 2. 12

NOTE, (i) (law) 'abstract of essential particulars relating to transfer of land by process of Fine, which was engrossed and placed on record' (O.E.D. sb.², 12), (b) observation; 2. 3. 124; (ii) notice, knowledge; 4. 1. 45

NOTED, (a) set to music, (b) notorious; 5. 2. 12

NUMBERS, metre, poetry; 3. 2. 182

OBJECT, spectacle, sight; 2. 2. 41; 3. 3. 180; 4. 5. 106

OBLIGATION, bond, tie; 4. 5. 122

OBSERVANCE (OF), reverence (for); 1. 3. 31; 2. 3. 163

OBSERVANT, attentive; 1. 3. 203

OBSERVING, attentive, deferential; 2. 3. 127

ODD, (i) (a) strange, (b) single, without a partner; 4. 5. 41, 42, 44; (ii) at variance; 4. 5. 265

ODDLY, unequally, incongruously; 1. 3. 339

ODDS, superiority (in numbers); 5. 4. 21

O'ERGALLÈD, fretted away, worn out; 5. 3. 55

O'EREATEN, eaten prodigally 5. 2. 160 (see note)

O'ERWRESTED (cf. WREST), strained, exaggerated; 1. 3. 157

OLD, (a) in years, (b) in experience; 1. 2. 118

OLYMPIAN, Olympic; 4. 5. 194

OPEN, (a) frank, (b) accessible to all; 5. 2. 25

OPINION, (i) public opinion; 1. 3. 142, 186; (ii) reputation; 1. 3. 336, 353, 372; 3. 3. 263; 4. 4. 103; 5. 4. 16

OPPOSED, facing one another; 3. 3. 107; 4. 5. 94

OPPRESS, overwhelm; 4. 5. 241

OPPUGNANCY, conflict; 1. 3. 111

ORCHARD, garden (not necess. with fruit trees); 3. 2. S.D., 16

ORDER, (i) plan, arrangement; 1. 3. 181; (ii) mode of procedure, regulation; 4. 5. 70, 90

ORGULOUS, proud; Prol. 2

ORIFEX. The common but erroneous form of 'orifice'; 5. 2. 151

ORTS (usu. in pl.), scraps of food left over; 5. 2. 158

OUT, (a) not in, (b) expired; 1. 2. 258

OUT, interjection expressing abhorrence; 5. 1. 34

OVERBULK, surpass in size, overgrow; 1. 3. 320

OVERHOLD, over-estimate; 2. 3. 132

OVERSHINE, outshine, surpass; 3. 1. 159

OWE, own; 3. 3. 99

OYEZ, the public cryer's call (Fr. oyez=hear) to command

silence and attention; 4. 5. 143 (see note)

PAGEANT (sb.), theatrical show, spectacle; 3. 2. 74; 3. 3. 271

PAGEANT (vb.), mimic; 1. 3. 151

PAINTED, 'painted cloth', see CLOTH; 5. 10. 45

PALATE, perceive (by taste); 4. 1. 61

PALE, paling, fence; 2. 3. 246

PALSY (adj.), palsied, shaky; 1. 3. 174

PALSY (sb.), paralysis; 'cold palsies'=paralysis induced by cold phlegm (see LETHARGY); 5. 1. 19

PALTER, play fast and loose; 2. 3. 230; 5. 2. 49

PARADOX, 'make paradoxes' =turn into absurdities; 1. 3. 184

PARD, leopard, panther; 3. 2. 193

PART (sb.), (i) portion, share; 1. 3. 352; (ii) inherent gifts, talents; 2. 3. 239; 3. 3. 117; 4. 4. 79; (iii) parts of the body; 2. 3. 247; (iv) party, side; 4. 5. 156; 5. 8. 15

PARTED, gifted, talented; 3. 3. 96

PARTIAL, personal; 2. 2. 178 (see note)

PARTICULAR (adj.), individual, personal; 1. 2. 20; 1. 3. 341; 2. 2. 53; 4. 5. 20

PARTICULAR (sb.), (i) item; 1. 2. 115; (ii) personal concern; 2. 2. 9

PASH, bash, batter; 2. 3. 201; 5. 5. 10

PASS, (i) 'it passed'=passed description, beat everything;

1. 2. 168; (ii) experience, undergo; 2. 2. 139

PASSAGE, course, progress; 2. 3. 130

PAST-PROPORTION, immensity; 2. 2. 29

PATCHERY, trickery, roguery; 2. 3. 70

PAVEMENT, paved thoroughfare (for all traffic); 3. 3. 162

PAVILION, tent (usu. of a stately kind); Prol. 15

PECULIAR, belonging to oneself, individual; 2. 3. 164

PEEVISH, senseless; 5. 3. 16

PELTING, paltry; 4. 5. 267

PER SE, by himself, unique; 1. 2. 15

PERFECTION, performance, achievement; 3. 2. 85, 91

PERSISTIVE, steadfast; 1. 3. 21

PERSON, personal appearance; 1. 2. 193; 4. 4. 79

PERSUADE, plead, expostulate; 5. 3. 30

PERTLY, boldly; 4. 5. 219

PETTISH, petulant, ill-humoured; 2. 3. 129

PHOEBUS, the sun god, the sun; 1. 3. 230

PHRYGIAN, of Phrygia (the part of Asia Minor in which Troy was situated), Trojan; 4. 5. 186, 223; 5. 10. 24

PHYSIC, dose with medicine, (esp.) purge; 1. 3. 377

PIA MATER, (transf.) brain; 2. 1. 70

PIECE, (a) cask of wine or brandy, (b) contemptuous term for a woman; 4. 1. 64

PIECE OUT, mend; 3. 1. 52

PIGHT, pitched; 5. 10. 24

PIN, type of something trifling; 5. 2. 23

PLACKET, (fig. contemptuously) woman; 2. 3. 20

PLANTAGE, plants; 3. 2. 176 (see note)

PLEASANT, merry, playful; 3. 1. 63

PLEASURE, (i) (a) wish, command, (b) enjoyment; 3. 1. 24; (ii) 'you speak your fair pleasure'=you are too kind (Schmidt); 3. 1. 49

PLIGHT, pledge; 3. 2. 160

PLUTO, god of Hades; 3. 3. 197 (see note); 4. 4. 127; 5. 2. 103

POINT, summit; 'at ample point'=to the full; 3. 3. 89

POISE (sb.), weight; 1. 3. 207

POISE (vb.), weigh, balance; 1. 3. 339

POLICY, (i) conduct of affairs; 1. 3. 197; (ii) cunning, strategy; 4. 1. 20; 5. 4. 9, 12; (iii) established system of government; 5. 4. 16

PORPENTINE, porcupine; 2. 1. 25

PORRIDGE, soup, broth; 1. 2. 243

PORT, gate (usu. of a walled town); 4. 4. 111, 136

PORTLY, imposing (O.E.D. 1); 4. 5. 162

POSITION, general proposition (O.E.D. 1); 3. 3. 112

POSITIVE, absolute; 2. 3. 64

POSSESS, inform; 4. 4. 112

POSSESSED, controlled by a demon or spirit, crazy; 2. 3. 168

POST, travel with the utmost speed; 1. 3. 93

POTATO-FINGER, finger exciting lust (the Spanish or sweet potato being reputed an aphrodisiac); 5. 2. 57

POWER, armed force; 1. 3. 139; 2. 3. 259

PREGNANT, apt; 4. 4. 88

PRENOMINATE, name beforehand; 4. 5. 250

PREPOSTEROUS, unnatural; 5. 1. 23

PRESENCE, demeanour; 3. 3. 269

PRESENTLY, immediately; 2. 3. 138; 4. 3. 6

PRETTY, ingenious; 1. 2. 156

PREVENTION, precaution; 1. 3. 181

PRICK, mere point, particle; 1. 3. 343

PRIMITIVE, earliest, original; 5. 1. 53

PRIMOGENITIVE, right of primogeniture; 1. 3. 106 (see note)

PRIZE, (a) thing of value, (b) booty; 2. 2. 86

PROCESS, course, tenor; 4. 1. 9

PROFESS, make a business of; 3. 3. 268

PROMPT, ready, disposed; 4. 4. 88

PROMPTED, eager; 5. 2. 175

PROOF, (i) test, trial; 1. 2. 130; 1. 3. 34; (ii) fulfilment; 5. 5. 5, 29

PROPEND, incline; 2. 2. 190

PROPENSION, inclination; 2. 2. 133

PROPER, (i) handsome; 1. 2. 193; (ii) one's own; 2. 2. 89

PROPORTION, (i) due relationship; 1. 3. 87; (ii) see also PAST-PROPORTION; 2. 2. 29

PROPOSE, set before one's mind, expect, look for; 2. 2. 146

PROPOSED, intended; 3. 2. 13

PROPOSITION, project; 1. 3. 3

PROPUGNATION, defence; 2. 2. 136

PROTEST, protestation (O.E.D. 1); 3. 2. 174

PROTRACTIVE, protracted; 1. 3. 20

PROVIDE, prepare, make ready; 3. 2. 210

PUBLICATION, announcement; 1. 3. 326

PUBLISH, proclaim; 5. 2. 113, 119

PUN, early var. of 'pound'; 2. 1. 38

PURPOSE, import intent; 1. 3. 264

PURSUE, (i) follow with hostility, continue the fight; 4. 5. 69; (ii) follow as a suppliant, entreat; 5. 3. 10

PURSUIT, endeavour; 2. 2. 142; 4. 1. 20

PUSH, attack, onset; 2. 2. 137

PUT BACK, thrust back; 4. 4. 34

PUTTOCK, bird of prey akin to the kite; 5. 1. 60

QUAIL, (transf.) loose woman; 5. 1. 51

QUALIFY, moderate; 2. 2. 118; 4. 4. 9

QUALITY, (i) nature, cause; 4. 1. 46; (ii) natural gifts; 4. 4. 76

QUESTION, conversation; 4. 1. 13

QUOTE, (orig. to mark a book with numbers, as of chapters, etc.) mark, scrutinize; 4. 5. 233

RANK (adj.), (i). gross, foul; 1. 3. 73; (ii) luxuriant in growth; (fig.) 1. 3. 318; (iii) intemperate; 4. 5. 132

RANK (adv.), excessively; 1. 3. 196

RANSACK, carry off as plunder; Prol. 8; 2. 2. 150

RAPE, seizure by force; 2. 2. 148

RAPTURE, transport, delirium; 2. 2. 122; 3. 2. 129

RASH, urgent; 4. 2. 60

RATE, chide, exclaim against; 2. 2. 89

REACH, scope; 4. 4. 108

RECORDATION, reminder; 5. 2. 116

RECOURSE, repeated flowing; 5. 3. 55

RECREANT, villain; 1. 3. 287

RED, applied to various diseases marked by evacuation of blood or cutaneous eruptions; 2. 1. 19 (see note)

REDEEM, (a) (law) free (mortgaged property), recover (a pledge), (b) liberate; 5. 5. 39

REFUSE, renounce; 4. 5. 267

REGARD, (i) glance, look; 3. 3. 41, 254; (ii) estimation; 3. 3. 128

REIN, 'in such a rein'=(fig.) in the same way; 1. 3. 189

REJOINDURE, reunion; 4. 4. 36

RELATION, report; 3. 3. 201

REPINING, grudging; 1. 3. 243

REPROOF, refutation; 1. 3. 33

REPURÉD, 'thrice repuréd'= purified thrice over; 3. 2. 22

RESPECT, reflection; 2. 2. 49

RESTY, restive; 1. 3. 263

RETIRE (sb.), retreat; 5. 3. 53; 5. 4. 19; 5. 8. 15

RETIRE (vb.), return; 1. 3. 281

RETORT, throw back, reflect; 3. 3. 101

RETREAT, signal (usu. by drums) for cessation of hostilities; 1. 2. 177 S.D. etc.

REVERSION, (a) (*law*) 'the return of an estate to the donor or grantor, or his heirs, after the expiry of the grant' (O.E.D. 1), (b) expectation; 3. 2. 91

RHEUM, mucous discharge; 5. 3. 104 (cf. note to 5. 1. 17–18)

RIVELLED, wrinkled; 5. 1. 22

ROISTING, roistering, uproarious; 2. 2. 208

ROUNDED IN, encompassed; 1. 3. 196

ROUNDLY, straightforwardly; 3. 2. 153

RUB, (i) 'rub the vein of him' =encourage his humour; 2. 3. 198; (ii) 'rub on', a cry encouraging a bowl on its course past a 'rub' (=obstacle); (fig.) 3. 2. 49

RUDE, (i) harsh, discordant; 1. 1. 91; (ii) brutal; 1. 3. 115; (iii) unskilled, inexperienced; 3. 1. 57; 3. 2. 25

RUDELY, roughly; 4. 4. 35

RUDENESS, violence; 1. 3. 207

RULE, (i) (a) carpenter's rule, (b) line of conduct; 5. 2. 133; (ii) law, principle; 5. 2. 141

RUN, (a) exude pus, (b) run away; 2. 1. 5, 6

RUTHFUL, lamentable; 5. 3. 48

SACRED, (an epithet of royalty) revered; 4. 5. 134

SAGITTARY, centaur; 5. 5. 14. (see note)

SALT, (fig.) stinging, bitter; 1. 3. 370

SANCTIMONY, (i) sacred thing; 5. 2. 139; (ii) sanctity; 5. 2. 140

SARSENET, fine, soft silk fabric, originally made by the Saracens (see Linthicum, pp. 121–2), here contemptuously used for slightness; 5. 1. 30

SAUCY, presumptuous; 1. 3. 42

SAVAGE, uncivil (Schmidt); 2. 3. 125

SCAB, (a) usu. sense, (b) (transf.) scurvy fellow; 2. 1. 28

SCAFFOLDAGE, platform, stage; 1. 3. 156

SCALÉD, with fish scales; 5. 5. 22 (see note)

SCANT, stint; 4. 4. 47

SCANTLING, sample; 1. 3. 341

SCAPE, escape; 1. 3. 371

SCAR, cut, incision (O.E.D. sb.^{2}); 1. 1. 113

SCHOOL, university; 1. 3. 104

SCREECH-OWL, barn owl, supposed a bird of ill omen; 5. 10. 16

SCRUPLE, (i) hesitation, objection; 4. 1. 58; (ii) (of diff. etymol.) the third part of a drachm; 4. 1. 72

SCULL, old form of 'school' (of fish); 5. 5. 22

SCURRIL, scurrilous; 1. 3. 148

SEAM, fat; 2. 3. 183

SEAT, seat of office, throne, (fig.) position of authority; 1. 3. 31

SECOND; 'in second voice' =by proxy; 2. 3. 139

SECURE, over-confident; 2. 2. 15

SECURELY, over-confidently; 4. 5. 73

SEE, meet one another; 4. 4. 57

SEEDED, run to seed; 1. 3. 316

SEETHE, boil; (fig.) 3. 1. 41

SEIZURE, grasp; 1. 1. 59

SELD, seldom; 4. 5. 150

SELF-ADMISSION, self-approbation; 2. 3. 164

SELF-AFFECTED, self-loving, vain; 2. 3. 236

SELF-ASSUMPTION, presumption; 2. 3. 123

SENNET, trumpet or cornet fanfare for ceremonial entries and exits; 1. 3. S.D.

SENSE, (i) physical feeling; 2. 1. 21; (ii) emotional feeling; 4. 4. 4; (iii) mental perception; 4. 5. 54 (see note)

SEQUESTER, separate; 3. 3. 8

SERPIGO, creeping skin disease, esp. ringworm; 2. 3. 73

SET, (i) stake; Prol. 22; (ii) 'set...to'=pit...against; 2. 1. 85

SEVERAL (adj.), separate, individual; 2. 2. 124, 193

SEVERAL (sb.), individual quality; 1. 3. 180

SEVERALLY, separately; 4. 5. 274; 5. 3. 94 S.D.

'SFOOT (an oath), God's foot; 2. 3. 5

SHAME, (i) disgrace; 1. 3. 19; (ii) shyness, modesty (O.E.D. 1); 3. 2. 41

SHARE, (i) cut off, cleave; 1. 3. 366; (ii) participate in (quibbling on (i)); 1. 3. 367

SHARP, fierce; 5. 9. 10

10

SHE (sb.), woman; 1. 2. 289, 291

SHED, disperse, scatter; 1. 3. 319

SHIVER, fragment; 2. 1. 38

SHOEING-HORN, (fig.) (a) person used as a tool, (b) cuckold; 5. 1. 54

SHOULD, (i) could; 1. 2. 31; (ii) would; 1. 2. 102; 1. 3. 112, 114, 116, 118; 2. 2. 48

SHREWDLY, severely, grievously; 3. 3. 228

SHRILL FORTH, utter shrilly; 5. 3. 84

SIEVE, basket, receptacle for fragments; 2. 2. 71 (see note)

SINEW, (fig.) strength; 1. 3. 136, 143

SINISTER, (heraldic term) left; 4. 5. 128

SIRRAH, term of address to inferiors, esp. servants; 3. 2. 6

SITH, since; 1. 3. 13; 5. 2. 120

SKILLESS, ignorant; 1. 1. 12

SKITTISH, (i) lively; Prol. 20; (ii) fickle; 3. 3. 134

SLACK, slacken; 3. 3. 24

SLEAVE-SILK, filament of silk obtained by separating ('sleaving') a thicker thread, floss silk; 5. 1. 30

SLEEVELESS, (a) without the sleeve, (b) (fig.) useless; 5. 4. 8

SLIDE, skate; 3. 3. 215

SLIGHTLY, carelessly; 3. 3. 166

SLIP, escape (with quibble on 'slip'=counterfeit coin); 2. 3. 25

SLUTTISH, immoral; 4. 5. 62

SO, SO, exclam. of approval; 5. 5. 44

SODDEN (ppl. of 'seethe'), (*a*) boiled, (*b*) with allusion to 'stew'=hot bath (cf. SWEAT, STEWED); 3. 1. 42

SODDEN-WITTED, stupid; 2. 1. 42

SOFT (exclam.), stay, stop; 5. 3. 89; 5. 4. 16

SOILURE, dishonour; 4. 1. 58

SOL, the sun; 1. 3. 89

SOLE, solely; 1. 3. 244

SOMETIME, sometimes; 1. 3. 151

SOOTH, truth; 'good sooth', 'in good sooth' (assevera-tions)=indeed; 2. 1. 108; 3. 1. 57

SOP, piece of bread, or the like, dipped or steeped in liquid; 1. 3. 113

SORT (sb.), (i) lot; 1. 3. 375; (ii) manner, way; 4. 1. 25; 5. 4. 34; 5. 10. 5

SORT (vb.), suit, fit; 1. 1. 108

SOUND, utter; 4. 2. 109

SPECIALTY, (*law*) 'a special contract, obligation, or bond, expressed in an instrument under seal' (O.E.D. 7); (fig.) 1. 3. 78

SPECULATION, sight, vision (O.E.D. 1); 3. 3. 109

SPEED, succeed, prosper (O.E.D. 1); 3. 1. 143

SPEND, utter; 'spend his mouth' (said of hunting dogs on finding or seeing the game, O.E.D. 9*b*)=give tongue; 5. 1. 88

SPERR, fasten with a bar or bolt, secure; Prol. 19

SPHERÉD, rounded; 4. 5. 8

SPLEEN, considered as the seat of the emotions; (i) laughter; 1. 3. 178; (ii) courage; 2. 2. 128; (iii) anger; 2. 2. 196

SPOTTED, polluted; 5. 3. 18

SPRIGHTLY, high-spirited; 2. 2. 190

SQUARE, take the measure of (with allusion to 'square'=instrument for testing right angles), judge; 5. 2. 132

STAIN, tinge; 1. 2. 25

STALE, make common, spoil; 2. 3. 189

START, (i) leap, bound; Prol. 28; (ii) startle; 5. 2. 102

STARTING, bounding; 4. 5. 2

STARVE OUT, endure in perishing cold (O.E.D.); 5. 10. 2 (see note)

STARVED, famished, (fig.) feeble; 1. 1. 95

STATE, (i) council of state; 1. 3. 191; 2. 3. 108, 257; 4. 2. 67; 4. 5. 65, 264; (ii) Government; 3. 3. 196, 202

STAY, wait (for); 3. 2. 3, 10

STEWED, (*a*) cooked by sim-mering, (*b*) with allusion to 'stew'=brothel; 3. 1. 42

STICK, stab; 3. 2. 194

STICKLER-LIKE, like an umpire; 5. 8. 18

STILL (adv.), constantly, al-ways; 3. 3. 22, etc.

STINT, stop, check; 4. 5. 93

STITHY, forge; 4. 5. 255

STOMACH, appetite, inclination; 2. 1. 124; 3. 3. 220; 4. 5. 264

STOOL, privy; 2. 1. 41

STRAIGHT (adv.), immediately; 1. 3. 389; 3. 2. 17, 31; 3. 3. 305; 4. 4. 144

STRAIN (sb.), (i) 'make no strain but that'=take it for granted that; 1. 3. 326; (ii) (of diff. etymol.) disposition; 2. 2. 154

STRAIN AT, find difficulty in, boggle at (cf. Matth. xxiii. 24); 3. 3. 112

STRAINED, purified as by filtering; 4. 4. 24; 4. 5. 169

STRANGE, (i) aloof; 2. 3. 236; (ii) new, alien; 3. 2. 9; 3. 3. 12

STRANGELY, aloofly; 3. 3. 39, 71

STRANGENESS, aloofness; 2. 3. 125; 3. 3. 45, 51

STRAWY, like straw; 5. 5. 24

STRIKE, (i) 'strike off'=cancel; 2. 2. 7; 3. 3. 29; (ii) beat a drum, etc.; 5. 10. 30

STUBBORN, (i) stiff; 3. 1. 151; (ii) ruthless, harsh; 5. 2. 131

STYGIAN, of Styx (the river of Hades across which the dead were ferried by Charon); 5. 4. 18

SUBDUEMENT, conquest; 4. 5. 187

SUBSCRIBE, (i) assent to; 2. 3. 146; (ii) yield; 4. 5. 105

SUBTLE, difficult, intricate; 4. 4. 87; (ii) fine, delicate; 5. 2. 151

SUCCESS, upshot, result; 1. 3. 340; 2. 2. 117

SUCH ANOTHER, (contemptuously) like any other; 1. 2. 259 (see note), 272

SUDDENLY, at once; 4. 4. 33

SUFFER, allow, permit; 4. 2. 30

SUFFERANCE, endurance, submission; 1. 1. 30; 2. 1. 95

SUFFOCATE, suffocated; 1. 3. 125

SUPERFICIALLY, (a) by sight, (b) slightly; 3. 1. 10

SUPPOSE, expectation; 1. 3. 11

SURETY, (i) security, guarantee; 1. 3. 220; 5. 2. 61; (ii) sense of security; 2. 2. 14, 15

SURLY, arrogantly; 2. 3. 235

SWAGGER, bluster, rant; 5. 2. 136

SWEAT, take the sweating treatment for venereal disease; 5. 10. 54

SYMPATHISE, agree; 4. 1. 27

TABLE, writing tablet, notebook; 4. 5. 60

TABORIN, 'a kind of drum, less wide and longer than the tabor, and struck with one drumstick only, to accompany the sound of a flute which is played with the other hand' (O.E.D.); 4. 5. 275

TAKE, strike with disease; 5. 1. 23

TAINT (sb.), disgrace; 1. 3. 373

TAINT (vb.), (a) strike, (b) infect; 3. 3. 232

TAME, familiar, acquainted; 3. 3. 10

TAMÉD, broached (like a cask); 4. 1. 64

TARRE ON, incite; 1. 3. 391

TASTE (vb.), (fig.) put to the proof, test; 1. 3. 337; 3. 2. 90

TAX, (i) censure; 1. 3. 197; (ii) order, enjoin; 5. 1. 40

TEMPER, disposition; 1. 3. 57

TEMPERED, composed, disposed; 2. 3. 251; 5. 3. 1

TEMPT, make trial of, risk; 4. 4. 96; 5. 3. 34

TEND, TEND ON, wait upon; 2. 3. 125; 4. 4. 146; 5. 1. 70

TENT, lint used to probe and cleanse a wound; 2. 2. 16; (with a quibble) 5. 1. 10

TERCEL, male of the falcon (q.v.); 3. 2. 52

TETTER, skin eruption; 5. 1. 22

THERE, a cry of encouragement; 5. 5. 43

THETIS, sea-nymph, daughter of Nereus and mother of Achilles, used, by metonymy, for the sea through confusion (even in Latin times) with Tethys, wife of Oceanus; 1. 3. 39

THICK (adv.), fast; 3. 2. 36

THIEVERY, things stolen; 4. 4. 43

THRIFTY, worthy; (iron.) 5. 1. 54

THROUGH, thoroughly; 2. 3. 220

THWART, athwart; 1. 3. 15

TIDE, opportune time; 5. 1. 81

TIME, period of gestation; 1. 3. 313

TIRED, exhausted; 3. 2. 175

TISICK, consumptive cough; 5. 3. 101

TITAN, Hyperion, the sun-god, the sun; 5. 10. 25

TO, a cry of encouragement; 2. 1. 108

TOAST, piece of toast often put into liquor; 1. 3. 45

TOPLESS, supreme; 1. 3. 152

TORTIVE, distorted; 1. 3. 9

TO'T, to the point; 3. 1. 31

TOUCH (sb.), (i) feeling; 2. 2. 115; 4. 2. 97; (ii) trait; 3. 3. 175

TOUCH (vb.), land at; 2. 2. 76

TRADED, skilled, practised; 2. 2. 64

TRAIN, induce; 5. 3. 4

TRANSLATE, interpret, explain; 4. 5. 112

TRANSPORTANCE, conveyance; 3. 2. 11

TRIM, excellent, fine; (iron.) 4. 5. 33

TRUE, (a conventional epithet for a sword) trusty; 1. 3. 238; 5. 3. 56

TRUMPET, trumpeter; 1. 3. 256, 263; 2. 1. 122; 4. 5. 6

TRUNCHEON, staff carried as symbol of office, e.g. by the arbitrator in a fight to give the signal for the beginning or cessation of hostilities; 5. 3. 53

TUCKET, short fanfare on a trumpet; 1. 3. 212 S.D.

TURTLE, turtle dove; 3. 2. 177

TWAIN, parted, estranged; 3. 1. 102

TYPHON, myth. monster with a tremendous voice; 1. 3. 160

UNBODIED, incorporeal; 1. 3. 16

UNBRUISÉD, unwounded; Prol. 14

UNCOMPREHENSIVE, unfathomable; 3. 3. 198

UNDERWRITE, subscribe to, submit to; 2. 3. 127

UNJUST, false; 5. 1. 87

UNKIND, unnatural; 3. 2. 148

UNPLAUSIVE, disapproving; 3. 3. 43

UNRESPECTIVE, undiscriminating; 2. 2. 71

UNSQUARED, rough (fig. from the mason's preparation of building stone); 1. 3. 159

UNTIMBERED, frail (cf. *Oth.* G. 'timbered'); 1. 3. 43

UNTRADED, unfamiliar; 4. 5. 178

UNWHOLESOME, foul, dirty; 2. 3. 119

USE (sb.), practice, habitual exercise; 5. 6. 16